Communicating with Grace

THE AWAKENING OF A PSYCHIC MEDIUM

SUSAN ANDERSON

COMMUNICATING WITH GRACE © copyright 2005 by Susan Anderson. All rights reserved. No part of this book may be reproduced in any form whatsoever, by photography or xerography or by any other means, by broadcast or transmission, by translation into any kind of language, nor by recording electronically or otherwise, without permission in writing from the author, except by a reviewer, who may quote brief passages in critical articles or reviews.

Previously published:
ISBN-13: 978-1-59298-109-0
ISBN-10: 1-59298-109-7

ISBN-13: 978-0-9767054-5-1
ISBN-10: 0-9767054-5-1

Printed in the United States of America
Interior illustration, p. 229 by Charles A. Filius

First Printing: May 2005
Second Printing: May 2006

09 08 07 06 05   5 4 3 2

LCCN: 2007920248

Itasca Books

3501 Hwy 100 South
Suite 220
Minneapolis, MN 55416

Visit our website: *www.bridgingtwoworlds.net*

THIS IS A SPECIAL TWO PART DEDICATION

This book is dedicated to everyone this book touches…
May it shine a light that brings witness to your life!

The second part of the dedication is
in loving memory of my brother Wayne,
Who turned the light on once again
"Nope-a-Light-a-Broke-a-Nope"
and who has been the wind beneath my wings!

CONTENTS

FOREWORD

At first glance, one might surmise that Susan Anderson's book *Communicating with Grace* is a small text about one woman learning to harness her psychic abilities. But though it chronicles a single story, it represents a much larger phenomenon in American society today.

That phenomenon is often referred to as New Age theology. Most psychics, be they spiritual advisors, healers, or mediums, dislike the term since the information they use and reveal is not necessarily new and the phrase brings with it all sorts of kooky connotations. However, since no one as of yet has thought of a better term, it must remain.

It is currently an emerging movement whose effects may well be as significant as the liberalism of the 1960's and 1970's. It is rapidly making its presence felt in mainstream American society today.

If you think this a ridiculous notion, just visit any bookstore and look at the expanding shelves of new age texts. Not only are more and more people writing them, hundreds of thousands of individuals are reading them and embracing their values.

Why? Because it has the ability to help individuals live better lives. Ask Anderson what psychic development is really about and she'll tell you quite plainly it is about healing emotional wounds, repairing broken relationships, creating a greater emotional presence, offering insights into one's life, and validating an uncertain path.

Part of all of this involves eliminating childhood fears and healing long-festering wounds inflicted by parents, teachers, and institutions. This kind of trauma can tarnish a person's self esteem, even though the wound may have resulted from something entirely beyond that person's control.

Because of their limited knowledge of the adult world, however, children oftentimes take responsibility for what happens around them. When bad things happen, they feel that they are unworthy, unlovable, and can never measure up to the expectations of their parents. So, one of Susan's ideals is that we, as adults, take responsibility for our own lives and own our own power. A person cannot heal unless he owns his own power, since he may still be holding onto perceptions he mistakenly had as a child. These false perceptions need to be healed.

Forgiving those who have trespassed against you, as the Lord's Prayer suggests, is an essential part of the healing process. As human beings, we have free will and, by cultivating our free will, we can make a conscious choice to evolve.

A generation of mostly female practitioners, including Anderson, has emerged. They mirror the emergence of female clergy in America, once prohibited but now considered a commonplace. But these psychics are not like ordained clergy; they are more like Old Testament prophets offering a kinder, gentler, individualistic alternative to the religious traditions that have dominated western civilization since its inception.

For someone like Anderson who is confronted with the relentless spiritual forces in their lives, there are very few places to turn to. Rabbis, priests, and ministers are often not equipped to deal with such issues, since their main job as spiritual leaders is to defend the religious dogmas of their faith. The issues of mediumship and psychic development stand outside the pale.

Individuals with Anderson's abilities are mentioned in both the Old and New Testaments. However, such references are often accompanied by warnings against the very activities she has mastered and her clients have come to trust. Unfortunately, since she has no advanced degree in medicine, psychology or theology, she is dismissed by many as fraudulent. However, she is not.

Part of what her story represents is the idea of a progressive revelation, the idea that our notion of divinity enlarges as we grow older as individuals and as a society, and is moving to a new place. In this new place, different faiths find common ground, and the notion of who we are in relation to God, our ancestors, our nation, and the human race as a whole expands.

As a medium, Anderson's psychic readings reveal the presence of spirits from the other side of the veil that separates mortals from the spiritual realm. But who comes forth is not Moses, Jesus, Mohammed, or Buddha, castigating individuals to embrace a stricter morality. Instead, the spirits who come are mothers and fathers, children, sisters and brothers, and grandparents of the individual she is reading.

Their intention is not to haunt or indict, but to help alleviate the conflict and guilt unresolved in their relationships when they were alive. That her mediumship always brings forth loved ones speaks to the fact that family love transcends death.

We might draw certain conclusions about the relationship between the dead and the living. Ironically, while we often feel pity for the dead, Anderson claims that she has never met a spirit pining for the warmth of a physical life. Messages from the other side always seem to suggest that existence is easier when one dies, and that the real struggles is the burden of mortal flesh.

Ask Anderson and she will tell you that what she sees are not mournful ghosts. In her experience, she has yet to find a spirit that prefers the trials and tribulations of the mortal world to the peaceful life on the other side. Sympathy, she said, should be offered to the living, because it is in this life that pain exists and not the life of the dead who have transcended.

Anderson's work is intended to help people become aware of the unrecognized spiritual component of their lives, a part that may lay dormant because of a lack of confidence in their own intuition, or because they fear that, by engaging in such communication with the dead, they will violate some religious commandment. Ultimately, however, it is by her fruits that she must be judged.

For Anderson, who is fifty-five years old, her sixth sense is a gift she has had since her childhood days in Plainview, Minnesota. Her book, as with all things psychic, has one purpose: it attempts to expand our understanding of the spiritual beyond the narrow confines of everyday life.

Is it really so hard to imagine that one's dead mother should appear to express her love, or offer regret for a problem-ridden relationship now better understood since she has passed?

How about a message from a dead son that he regrets the choices he made in life and that, in his current place, he is safe and sound?

What is striking about Anderson's readings is not so much that spirits give mortals advice about how to live their lives, but that they seemed to know as much, if not more, about the life of the individual they cared about. In many cases, those who have passed have a clearer insight to the issues that trouble the living person him or herself.

Do dead relatives actually know more about a person's earthly contract from beyond the veil than does the individual himself?

"Yes," Anderson said. "They have greater access to a person's higher self than do most of us on this side."

When reading, she seeks a validation, a message from a spirit that is usually so private that only the recipient of it would know it to be true. Its purpose is to prove that Anderson is in contact with a spirit closely related to the individual for whom she is doing the reading.

When communicating with spirits, Anderson finds that their purpose is to offer a sense of understanding. None are telling relatives to call their brokers and buy Pfizer stock, bet on the Minnesota Vikings on Monday Night Football, or invest in real estate. The current mania for money and fame is not what they value. Their intention is to offer information that will help us live a more peaceful and graceful life.

"It is about healing, understanding, and evolution," Anderson said. "It is difficult for someone to move on through life and evolve unless we are willing to let go of hurts, frustrations and anger that someone has chosen to hang on to. It's about connecting with spirit and being able to let go of those feelings that held us back."

Communicating with Grace focuses on self-development, self-examination, and self-help. Perhaps by understanding her passage, your own anxiety level might go down, and your life might become more hopeful. You might also become a bit more detached, with more energy, grace, and better yet, more loving relationships.

Individuals like Anderson are trying to bring these values into the mainstream and in this new millennium, which can be characterized by the urges of globalization and multiculturalism, it could be the recipe that helps us, as a species, evolve to a higher level.

Her ethical outlook is a fine accompaniment to twenty-first century life, because it focuses on what is innate in people and does not separate them according to race, religion, or nationality.

Individual psychic development is a process which can help us evolve as a species. The emerging spirituality of this new age will have a lasting effect on American society and will one day be seen as commonplace for a whole generation of American adults.

In that effort, Anderson is at the vanguard.

—*Bob Gilbert*

ACKNOWLEDGMENTS

I would like to offer a special thanks to my husband, **Jeffrey**, who has the wisdom, foresight, and patience to allow me the space and support I need to grow and develop. Thank you for trusting our relationship and having faith in me, especially when I was tired and hesitated...*I LOVE YOU!*

Christine Anderson: A special acknowledgement to my daughter. Here's to the past that we have been through together, the present that I enjoy with you, and the future that we will share. I offer you a heartfelt and respectful thank you. I can only imagine how many lifetimes we've had, and will have, together!

Our company Introspect...A Look Within, exists because of you. The work we have done and will do exits because of your unshakeable faith, tenacity and insights. I am doing this work because you envision, nurture, and support the possibilities of today and tomorrow! You are heaven-sent. The wisdom you apply in your work is proof that you are wise beyond your years.

I've enjoyed the journeys we have taken and will take with Friar and Charlie beside us. Just as Louisiana, New York, Chicago, Texas, Florida, and Tennessee are part of our past together, so many other places are in our future! Blessings to you for all you are and will become!

My Sons, Steven and David: Blessings and love for being a part of my life. It hasn't been an easy road. Thank you for reminding me that there is a lighter side to life. Your strengths give me a reflective view of the possibilities I see. Always with love!

Wayne: In life, you turned the light on, and from the other side you turned it on once again…..Nope-a-Light-a-Broke-a-Nope.

Thank you for putting my hand in Friar's and for being there. In life, you lived the example and on the other side you are the wind that lifts me, causing me to soar. You are always in my heart and a gift from above.

Friar: My life guide and leader of "the Team." I offer deep gratitude for your loving grace, wisdom, and guidance. It is your hard work and dedication that keeps me whole. You believed in me when I didn't, encouraged me when I doubted, and, through your guidance, brought me what I needed so that I could take those leaps of faith. Thank you.

James: Thank you for being my life protector, for watching over me and bringing in protection for me when I needed it. You and Friar are my lifelines.

The Team: A thank you and acknowledgement to the thirty-six. Blessings to all of you who have been here, who are here, and who will come in to help when it is needed. You are the members of the boardroom.

John Edwards: You shine like a beacon for so many. It is your dedication to the process and your willingness to step out front and center that sets a high standard for this work. It is your life's work that brought me to mine. Thank you, John.

Lydia Clar: I offer you gratitude for help and guidance through my rite of passage. It was a difficult time and I am grateful that you were there. Your skills are heaven-sent and appreciated more than words could express. I look forward to the rest of the journey with your guidance.

Patti Star: My star of aromatherapy and massage using pure essential oils. You taught me to connect my head and heart and, in turn, helped me receive the true messages I needed to make myself whole.

The love you show for your work and your clients is inspiring. You've taught me to always look for the possibilities and I cherish your friendship. Gratitude and blessings, dear friend and mentor.

Thank you for mixing those special blends and for the work you have done for all of us, students and family included. The knowledge you bring into the classroom, as well as your dedication and love, is greatly appreciated.

Bob Gilbert: This book would not be what it is if it hadn't been for you. Thank you for being a trusted friend and supporter of this work. In honor of your willingness to "be there" and to provide the dedication it took to help me bring this book into being, I offer you blessings and gratitude. I look forward to a long and continued friendship. And yes, forever young!

April Rogoyski: It was a learning experience meeting you. The discoveries we've made along the way have validated so much for each of us. I look forward to seeing the rest of your journey unfold as we each walk our own path. Thank you for being a deeply-trusted friend, and for the faith, laughter, and tears, we've shared. The journey would not be complete without you. I am still waiting for the "beaded bag."

Mic McManus: My shamanic healer, guide, and dear friend. Thank you for the time we've shared, for allowing me to walk alongside you, and for sharing your time and special gifts with me. You taught me that it was okay to trust my heart and to be brave enough to let go of things that no longer had importance. Your gentle words I hold in my heart even today, and I am grateful. Thank you for teaching me to trust myself, to keep in my life what resonates and to let go of what does not.

In moments of happiness or great distress, this is what has helped me bring balance in my life. Blessings and an offering of gratitude to you for the love, wisdom, and guidance you shared with me.

Sandy Anastasi: Even though I was already a psychic medium, I learned from your classes and dedication "why" I could do what I do and how I could harness my abilities in a way that keeps me safe and strengthens my skills.

It was you, my Mother Hen, who said, "You'd never let me hit the wall, but allow me to stub my toe." I believed in you. It was your belief in me that helped me believe in myself. Your mentorship means more to me than words could ever express. Your teaching skills and dedication inspired me. I cherish your friendship and the time we spent together. I send you a special thank you!

Starchild/Astrological Institute: The safe and protected environment that you offered allowed me the opportunity to discover the "why" of what I could do. The courses were a part of my foundation for this work. The experiences opened my eyes: I will always remember them! I offer you only the very best. Namasté.

Charles Filius: Thank you for sharing your creativity and other psychic mediumship gifts with me. You are gifted beyond words and your humor kept me on my toes. Thank you for the drawings and designs you have created. A heartfelt thank you for the picture of Friar that you created. The drawing touched my heart and the validation you provided me by bringing it into the physical world touched me deeply. Your gifts should be shared with the world.

A heartfelt thank you to Marian and family: Your presence is a continual sign that "Wayne was here." My brother made a wise choice for his life partner and wife. You are all loved!

Bonnie Wingness: Thank you for all the times you have been there for me to encourage and sometimes question me. You helped to bring understanding to the process I was going through. *Wash All My Cares Away* was an event that turned out to bring us closer and the result of the song is a validation that the shower is a great place to start with guidance, moves to your piano with guidance, and then brings validation to those beautiful moments of this journey that we shared. Thank you, sis.

Psychic Development Students: To those of you who shared classes with me, it was quite an experience. And to those students I met while auditing the classes at Starchild, and to my Psychic Development students, past, present, and future, a thank you for all that you share and teach the teacher!

Introspect's Students and Graduates: A special offering of gratitude to Introspect's 2003/2004 students and graduates. You gave us the inspiration to create the *Inner Journey*© and the *Bridging Two Worlds*© Series.

Ruth Koscielak and the staff at RBN Productions and www.ruthradio.com in Minneapolis, MN: Ruth, thank you for the opportunities you and Kel gave us and thanks to your listeners as well. James, thank you for the Rod Stewart songs! We have enjoyed being on your show and look forward to visits in the future.

Mori Studio: Thank you for all the dedication, knowledge and hard work that helped bring this project into the physical world. .

A thank you to those of you who have touched my life, including my family, friends, and acquaintances over the years. All of you have brought me to where I am today. Every one of you is important and remembered. If you ask yourself, "Could it be me?" the answer must be, "There is no doubt, IT IS!"

A SPECIAL ACKNOWLEDGEMENT

Thank you to the Father, Son, and Holy Spirit. You are, and always will be, a big part of my foundation. Thank you for your loving grace, guidance, and divine wisdom. To honor you does not limit me but only opens all possibilities.

I offer gratitude!

PREFACE

"The future will never be as important,
nor the past more important than, the present.
All are entwined, one the makeup of the other."

In the fall of 1954, our family was living in what we called the "Maiwald House" in Plainview, Minnesota. A friendly little man watched me play. He'd laugh when I pretended to ride imaginary horses and to chase imaginary butterflies.

I didn't realize then that this man had passed away on June 9, 1954. His name was Henry Maiwald. The feeling I got when I saw this man outside the house was much different than the feeling I had when I saw him inside. Inside the house, Henry seemed to have more of an agenda. When his wife came to collect the rent, I could feel his anger and would hear sounds similar to that of an iron dropping on the upstairs floor. Our dog, Skipper, would sit at the bottom of the stairs and howl.

Upstairs, I would feel a cold chill when, moving down the hallway, he passed through me. I would also feel him watching over me as I drifted off to sleep. I was only five years old and this is my earliest recollection of sensing people on the other side. And although it may seem eerie to some, back then I thought my experiences were no different from those of every body else.

Today, I am a professional psychic medium, teacher, and lecturer. I have done a tremendous amount of readings in person, over the phone, and on the radio, giving people messages from people who have crossed over to the other side. Whether it is from a child or adult, the message always has significance both for the person relaying it and the person on this side. Each reading has demonstrated to me that love does transcend death, and that the desire to bring understanding, to offer a greeting, or to heal a past issue for those here is just as important to those on the other side. It validates that life exists after death.

I often think about my growing up in that small town and how, until a few years ago, I had never had a reading or a healing. In fact, if someone had offered me one, I probably would have thought, "His elevator doesn't go to the top floor."

This book is about my personal journey. It tells of actual events from my point of view, and I've relayed them with as much accuracy as possible. Some students and clients have allowed me to share their experiences with my work, and I send a special "thank you" to each of them for being a part of the experience. Perhaps this book will spark an awakening in you, bring back a memory, raise a question, offer you validation or affirmation, or simply make you smile, laugh, and, perhaps once in a while, shed a tear or two.

In working in my chosen profession, I have learned to have a sense of humor. It's good to know that, when someone wants to poke fun at you or your journey, it is always about him or her and not about you. It generally gives us great material to discuss during class, especially when we are working on the section, "Owning Your Own Power."

Working through "Owning Your Own Power" is a huge lesson. When students learn the dynamics of this concept, they strengthen their sense of who they are and want to be. Mastering the art of taking responsibility for our choices in life—taking from each experience the positive aspects while letting go of the negative ones—is what frees us!

Publicly or privately acknowledging, or admitting, that I am a "psychic medium" has sparked all kinds of emotions and conversations among family, friends, and acquaintances. And as you read, you may discover yourself reacting in a similar way.

I have learned that having faith allows me to take one step at a time on the journey through this life. As the proverbial "they" say, "When God closes a door, he opens a window," but "they" never specify the length of time between the shuttings and the openings! Perhaps learning of the timeframe is part of the lesson of learning patience. And in my experience, a window has always opened, whether the door was only shut, was jammed, or was just plain dysfunctional.

I do thank "the man upstairs" for everything that has touched my life. The good, the bad, and the indifferent have indeed brought me to where I am today and will carry me to where I will need to be tomorrow. I am particularly grateful when the hardship is over and the lesson done, and I look forward to a time of learning with less pain! How about you?

PART I
the Awakening

DAYS *of* APRIL

*"There is a thin veil that exists between this life
and the other side. It can be just a fleeting moment when
we travel between the two dimensions and our world
is changed forever."*

I stood in my kitchen paralyzed with fear as I replayed in my head the vision that woke me. Around me, the morning activities appeared normal. My husband was in the other room on his cell phone and our Dalmatian, Josie, was outside on squirrel patrol. My daughter, Christie, had called to confirm she was stopping by: everything seemed normal.

Yet, the feeling of fear ran through me like bone-chilling water. The picture of my brother in a silvery-blue casket kept reappearing in my mind. Flowers the colors of spring—daisies, mums, carnations, roses, and peace lilies—were lined up in a single row at each end of the casket. He was wearing a grey suit and I saw a room with rows of chairs, filled with both family and people I did not know. It looked like a visitation or a funeral. With each reappearance of this vision, I would hear a voice saying repeatedly, "Can you ignore this now?" Tears streamed down my face and my heart felt like it was breaking as I answered again and again, "Yes, I can."

The oldest of my family siblings, Wayne, was born November 25, 1936. His great sense of humor and his ability to tease were his trademarks. I have so many fond memories of him.

When I was a child, I remember him playing the piano and trumpet. He played the piano and smiled as he sang "I Saw Mommy Kissing Santa Claus." I would start crying, saying, "My Mommy wouldn't do that!" I remember him singing "All I Want for Christmas is My Two Front Teeth" the year I was missing my two front teeth. As much as he teased, it was always with jovial laughter.

His nickname for me was "Susie Q," and when I would run and fall, he'd call me "Bambi on ice." Tall and with long legs, I was not the most graceful of young ladies. He always picked me up, dusted me off, and got me going again. He was my hero and my big brother. Wayne joined the Air Force in 1955 and retired in 1967. During his time in the Air Force, he married his hometown sweetheart, Marian Graner. While he was in the Air Force, I would look forward to his return. When I was old enough, I looked forward to visiting him and his wife. I loved helping with their children, too.

When he retired from the Air Force, he began his employment with Rockwell Collins in Cedar Rapids, Iowa. Wayne and Marian raised their five children, and he retired from Rockwell International in 1995.

After retiring, he moved to our home town of Plainview, Minnesota. He held a position on the City Council and lived there with Marian, his wife of forty-five years, until his death in 2002, at the age of sixty-five.

That day in the kitchen, the picture of Wayne in his casket and the accompanying words I heard returned frequently. I felt my heart breaking as I asked for them to stop, but from someplace deep inside me I understood that what I had seen was about to happen. My brother was alive now, and the feeling of "knowing" that he soon wouldn't be gave way to a feeling of dread.

I was excited that Christie, my daughter, was coming over later that morning. She had always been so adventurous and seemed to always rise to whatever challenges she met, even life's extraordinary ones. She began modeling in New York right out of high school. With very little money and a faith-filled heart, she modeled for two years before returning to Minnesota.

When she returned to Minneapolis, she felt it was time to get married and have children. She now lived in St. Paul where she was raising her family. We have always had a very close relationship and have been each other's confidant. We have always thought of one another, "No one can irritate me more, but I love you, anyway!" I don't think either of us can imagine life without the other. I knew I could share my experience of seeing the image of Wayne in a casket with her. Hopefully, she would come up with some brilliant explanation for it all, and bring me some temporary relief. I was hoping that talking with Christie would make everything seem a lot better. After all, she was the one into the weird psychic stuff, not me. I remember her telling me about a reading she gotten from Shelly Peck, a well-known psychic from Long Island, New York, as well as other readings she had received over the years. I always felt she was playing around; I didn't take the psychic stuff seriously at all.

When she arrived, I dragged her off to my bedroom immediately so that we could have a private conversation about this strange vision I had seen. She suggested I call Wayne to say hello and see if everything was okay. My call confirmed that Wayne and his family were fine. I hung up, feeling instant relief. I breathed a deep sigh of relief, but suddenly the vision reappeared, like a picture standing in front of me. I saw Wayne in his casket and again I heard that mild voice say, "Can you still ignore this?"

The feeling of dread quickly returned. I knew intuitively that this vision was revealing the truth and that Wayne would die. Though I knew it would happen, I did everything I could to run from this reality.

Christie was very supportive. She was quick to remind me that there was nothing I could do to change things if they were going to happen. Perhaps it was best to sit back and let the future unfold as it was intended to unfold. This, I learned, was not an easy thing to do.

During the next couple of days, whether I was waking up in the wee hours of the morning, taking a shower, cleaning the dishes in the kitchen, or having a conversation with someone, the vision of Wayne in his casket would appear unannounced and that gentle voice would always say, "Can you still ignore this?"

Christie and I stayed in close contact about what was happening. I wasn't able to shake the feelings, the picture, or the voice and I wondered if I was going crazy. On the one hand, part of me knew that this vision was revealing the truth and on the other hand, part of me was running scared. Christie was doing everything she could to reassure me that I was okay and this would pass.

On April 14th just four days after the visions started, the phone rang. It was my Mother. She said, "Last night Wayne was rushed by ambulance to St. Mary's Hospital in Rochester. It's his heart and he is not doing well." I hung up the phone and burst into tears. My vision of Wayne—his lying in the silvery-blue casket, the flowers lined up in a single row, the chairs forming rows in front of and to the side of the casket—reappeared. I could hear the voice again ask, "Can you still ignore this?" I felt as if my heart were being ripped out of my chest.

I had made every effort to be in denial of the truth of this vision. I didn't want to see or hear it and I certainly didn't want to believe that I had known about an event that was now taking place! But placing my head in the sand like an ostrich was not helping me a bit.

When a client now asks me if I know when someone they love might be passing, my heart aches as I remember the feelings of those days of April. I will not go there. What difference could my revealing the answer possibly make? We should all savor every day we have with those we love. Never pass up a chance to say, "I love you."

I called my husband to share the news. He was supportive, and I could hear the worry and concern in his voice as he suggested that I go to Rochester. We hung up, and I made arrangements to leave right away.

I called Christine and all she said was, "I'm so sorry, Mom." She offered to go to Rochester with me and, of course, I gladly accepted. She said she would get ready and come right over to the house.

Stunned with disbelief, I walked to my bedroom so that I could lie down for a few minutes. I felt almost as if I were out of my body. As I lay on the bed, I noticed that the television had been left on and a show called *Crossing Over* was playing. John Edward, a psychic medium and the show's host, was bringing in messages from deceased loved ones for members of his audience. I remembered the first time I had seen an episode. At the time I thought, "Wow, he looks normal and he gets paid for doing that?"

As I watched the television show, I felt my mind drifting away. With my mind's eye I was seeing flashbacks of my childhood in Plainview, Minnesota, a childhood that, for some reason, I had difficulty remembering and had to be reminded of by my siblings. As the memories unfolded one by one, I began to understand that I was starting to recall parts of my childhood that I had chosen to forget. As the visions played out, I recognized the common theme of my childhood: I had always felt that I was doing something wrong when I was "seeing" things psychically and that I would get in trouble for doing it.

In the first vision, I saw myself as a child walking into the living room. My mother was sitting on the sofa and my dad was standing beside her. He appeared to be comforting her; she seemed upset and was crying. My grandmother sat with her arms extended around my mother, as if to embrace her.

I asked my dad why Mom was crying. Dad acknowledged me, saying, "Because her mother died." I quickly replied, "Mom, don't cry; she is okay. She is right there." I saw her in plain view, in her dress and shoes, with a caring smile on her face as she caressed my mother's arms. My dad seemed very upset and sternly sent me to my room.

The second vision I had was of a funeral. A child friend of ours, Carol Binder, had passed away from complications due to a ruptured appendix. I remembered walking by the casket and seeing Carol lying there with her eyes shut, as if she were sleeping, holding a white book. As I glanced across the room, I also saw her sitting on the floor next to her mother. People were crying, but I couldn't understand why they were all sad. When I asked permission to go play with her, I was told very sternly, "No; please be still."

The third vision was of me seeing Edgar, the elderly gentleman who always bought us ice cream sundaes at the drug store after church. I saw myself bicycling away from his farm, bringing honey home for my mom. I also saw myself driving his tractor and listening to him playing his piano. Then the scenes changed. I was in my bed asleep and I was awakened by a dream of him driving down a highway outside of Plainview: I could see his car crash and feel his heart stop beating.

In the vision, I recalled the terrible feeling of being told the next morning that he had died in an auto accident and I would not be able to see him anymore. And although my parents told me "You won't see him anymore," it was my secret that I continued to see him at the drug store, and that he often walked with me to school. When I got a little older, he accompanied me on my bike rides out of town to go horse back riding. I didn't feel alone on those trips out to the farm.

The fourth vision was of me as a child, playing outside the "Maiwald House." Henry, the deceased gentleman who had lived there, would watch me play by what used to be a small barn. As a child, I liked him because he was friendly and would play with me outside.

On one of those days, I had brought a black cocker spaniel home. The dog had belonged to a school friend who was moving and couldn't take Skipper with her. I asked my mom if I could keep him and she said, "No, he's too dirty." Henry stayed outside the house with me while I waited for my dad to get home; I was hopeful that my dad would let me keep him. Henry told me not to worry, that I would get help. Shortly after, my sisters came home. Bonnie took the dog to the basement where she cleaned him up for me, making him presentable for my dad's pending arrival. Henry was right; with my dad's and my sister's help, my mother gave in and I was able to keep Skipper.

Remembering this event, I also recalled how strange it seemed that Henry was friendly to me, and that our dog liked him, when we were outside the house, but that things were very different when we were all inside the house.

Skipper would sit and howl at the bottom of the stairs. The dog would wait for one of us to go upstairs and would never go up by himself. Henry's bedroom must have been in the room where I slept, because he would be there, as if to watch over Skipper and me.

When Henry's wife, Katherine, came over to collect the rent, the dog would howl and I would always hear the sound of an iron falling on the floor above.

In a small town, homicides do not happen very often, and apparently there was talk around town of suspicious circumstances surrounding his death. Being only five years old, I didn't know this. I was never told how and why Henry died.

I recently looked up the information through the Minnesota Historical Society and received a copy of Henry's death certificate and of a Plainview newspaper from 1954. The headline read "Robert Stettler Pleads Guilty To Second Decree Manslaughter Charged In Death of Henry Maiwald." The article reported that Stettler had been charged with the fatal beating that took place on June 9. In the statement signed by Mr. Stettler, a step-grandson of Henry and a combat veteran, he said that he and Henry had gotten into an argument. According to court proceedings, Stettler struck Henry over the head with a broken beer bottle and Henry fell to the ground, alive but injured. Stettler went inside the house and returned outside, continuing the fight with the seventy-seven-year-old gentlemen. The article implied that his wife may have been at the farm during the murder. The article stated that Henry was survived by his wife, Katherine, a daughter, and one granddaughter.

The autopsy report reveals that Henry suffered a broken neck as well as a brain hemorrhage. Henry's daughter was the person who signed the death certificate. I now understand why Henry acted the way he did in the house when his wife came to call.

In the fifth vision, my grandfather was busy carrying a Christmas tree home. My grandparents always put the tree up on my birthday, December 16, and took it down on my sister Nancy's birthday, January 3. In the vision, I saw him sick and fragile. Upon returning home, he was lying on his sofa and Grandma was crying. The day of my birthday came and my parents received a phone call telling them that Grandfather was taken to Veteran's Hospital in Minneapolis, Minnesota. It was apparent that he had suffered a heart attack. We drove the 100-mile trip to see them. I remember sitting in the waiting room at the hospital, while some of the family was permitted up to his room to see him. He died shortly after his heart attack. I was five years old.

I now remember that, after his passing, I saw him many times at my grandmother's house. After his death, I could still feel him on the porch where my grandmother now cuddled me rather than him. The three of us would sit still, listening to the early morning songs of the birds. I could still see him at their house, sitting in his favorite chair as we worked on building a house of cards. I would hear his laughter as the cards tumbled to the ground.

I remember Grandma and me talking about how he was still there with her and how she, too, could hear what he was saying. At that time I began to realize that I felt safe connecting with people on the other side.

As the visions stopped, John Edward's show was still playing on the television and my daughter entered the room. We watched the last part of *Crossing Over* together and I shared with her what I had been seeing. I mentioned to her that John Edward had written a book. I asked her if she would like to go to the book store. She happily agreed. We purchased *One Last Time* and noticed that John Edward also had some audiotapes. We decided to buy the book first. It was the first book of its kind that I had ever purchased.

Christie and I drove to Rochester. I read the book from cover to cover while my brother was in the hospital. It made great material for conversation, and Christine and I shared many stories about past "events." I shared with her that, unlike others, I wasn't hopeful that Wayne would get well. I "knew" he would die. It was so painful to watch the family gather at the hospital and talk about all the things that were going to make him better. All I could do was smile and nod.

I told Christine that I had a feeling of being cheated, that I was jealous that they had all this hope and I didn't. The picture, or "vision," of Wayne's visitation kept reappearing every time someone told me that he would be okay.

When I entered Wayne's hospital room, he looked directly at me, though it felt as if he was looking through me. For some reason, his intense stare said more than words ever could. I knew that on some level he knew the same information I did. It was as if he was waiting for his grown children to gather and accept what was going to happen. Because of the size of our family and limited visitation privileges, I was not able to spend time alone with him, but it really didn't matter. I knew we shared a special connection.

My daughter and I drove home to Minneapolis. We had a lot of time together to talk about John Edward's book—Christie had read it by now, too—and about what was happening to Wayne. I made arrangements to return to Rochester as soon as I could.

My sister Nancy called to let us know that my younger brother, Jon, was coming into town. Jon is a ROTC graduate from the University of Minnesota, a retired Air Force pilot. and now works for a commercial airlines. He lives in Ohio with his wife Dianna and son, Lou. The thought of his arrival made my heart leap with excitement. Growing up in a large family of seven children wasn't always easy. My sibling position in the family is third youngest and Jon is one year younger than I am. The feelings I hold for my brother Jon are as warm as a sun shining on my face. I always look forward to his visits but certainly wished this time that it was under better circumstances.

It had been a while since our last visit and his upcoming arrival triggered some fond memories. I recalled that playing with him often entailed "making a deal." He would promise to play Barbie with me only if I agreed not to tell his friends and to play baseball with him later.

And then I remembered what is probably my favorite memory, about one of our stays at Grandma's house in Minneapolis. We had gotten our hands on a few firecrackers. We were in her basement when we had one of our brilliant ideas: we would light one, take it quickly outside, throw it, and listen to it pop. Well, as fate would have it, we were standing in the basement stairway and I was lighting the firecracker he was holding when my grandmother called from another room, "What are you kids doing?" At the same time, her brother stirred in his room, which was located in the basement right next to the stairway. We panicked and hesitated: not a good thing to do with a small fuse burning! The firecracker blew up in his hand. It left a black spot and, even though he was silent, I knew it had to sting. He sure was a good sport about it, though. Of course, we were asked about the noise. We never did admit to my grandmother what it was. This has now become one of our favorite family stories of times gone by.

I made a hotel reservation in Rochester so that I had a room next to my sister Nancy and her husband, John. Nancy is two years older then I. John was from our hometown area and married my sister in Plainview after they completed high school. Growing up, John lived with his deeply religious and disciplined family on a farm. John and Nancy have a large and united family. Religion has always been a very important part of their home.

The family spent time at the hospital with Wayne's children and shared a meal at a little pizza café in Plainview. That evening Nancy, her husband John, my brother Jon, and I spent a little time visiting with one another. Jon had to leave in the morning and I enjoyed the short walk he and I took back to his motel. It felt like old times and was very relaxing. When I returned to the hotel, Nancy and John were sitting, waiting for me. When I later explained to Christie what happened that evening, I said, "It struck terror in my heart."

Nancy, John, and I got into a conversation about what I had seen. I described the visions I had been having and told them about other people I had seen who had passed, such as my dad, who passed away in 1989.

I was not prepared for their reaction. John immediately stated sternly and authoritatively that I should not look at the other side, that is was important that I turn my head away. He declared that paying attention to people on the other side would open a door that would allow evil to come through. I felt the tug of war starting within me again. How could seeing my dad on the other side, feeling his warmth and love, smelling his cherry tobacco, and hearing his voice as we talked, be anything less than a gift?

My siblings and I were raised Lutheran, as was John, but my brother-in-law attended a different Lutheran church than my family had. John had often told stories about his painfully strict upbringing. He was never shy about discussing his belief system. Until this evening, though, I didn't realize how differently we perceived things. In my opinion, John and Nancy embraced a fear-based religion. I, on the other hand, must have been raised in a different time zone. As a child, I always felt that God protected me and that I didn't need to fear him because he loved me. And, just as I knew that my dad was there for our family, I thought that God as a father would always be there for me. Anything coming from God couldn't be evil.

My brother-in-law's comments that I was letting evil in when I paid attention to my psychic "seeings" made no sense to me. I never felt threatened in any way by the other side. I always felt loving grace. However, I soon learned that John's negative reaction was based on his own experiences with the other side.

He said he had also seen my dad on occasion, and that he felt my dad brought dark entities with him when he appeared. I told John that I didn't feel or see anything that matched his description. As his brown eyes darkened to almost black, he stated emphatically, "You are wrong! We had to have our daughter's place cleared because of Dad's visits there."

He told another story of visiting my dad's gravesite: something dark had jumped out at him and demanded that he leave. This story scared the bejeebers out of me. He seemed to be telling one of those "boogey man" Hollywood horror stories, but he was really referring to my own father. I couldn't believe it.

Dealing with John's hostile response was a new experience for me and I hadn't yet learned to stand up to something like this or to even know what really resonated for me. I had gotten so scared by John's stories that I asked John and Nancy to walk me back to my room to make sure it was empty and I was safe. All I could think of was the movie *Psycho*. I had a hard time sleeping that night. Believe me, the light stayed on all night!

Today, I remember this event and my brother-in-law's gravesite experience with a smile. My dad never liked John's "Reverend Mr. Black" attitude, so perhaps my dad purposefully "spooked" him. I would like to think that it is possible that he did that. After all, my dad probably would have enjoyed such a "joke," since he had a great sense of humor and he knew John's lack of humor where religion was concerned. I also now believe that John's own fear of the other world draws negativity to him, since my own experience has never been like his.

In the wee hours of the morning in the Rochester hotel though, I laid awake practicing the fine art of proving myself wrong. I tried to convince myself that John must be right, given how faithfully he practiced his religion. His being right left only one conclusion: I had to be wrong. The inner fight was on. In my heart, I knew what I had seen, but was choosing to renounce the truth that resonated with me in favor of what resonated with him. The cost of this would mount over the next weeks.

Wayne's doctors at St. Mary's decided to make an attempt at surgery, and were careful to explain to us that he was approaching death and his chance of surviving any procedure was very slim. It was when he was in the operating room that I first felt him pull away from and then get tugged back into his body. I later found out that they had a hard time reviving him during surgery and that his heart refused to beat independently of the equipment they used.

I wasn't at the hospital, but I could see him standing next to his wife, Marian, as she looked at him after surgery, his body attached to the life-support machines. While he was hooked up to the machines, I felt him finally break free; it was as if a great weight had been holding him down and all of a sudden he was propelled weightless into the air, elated to be free. They say his heart literally "fell apart bleeding." They couldn't keep him going.

My brother Wayne passed away on April 27. I will always remember feeling his pulling away when his spirit left his body.

I called my mom to ask her if she knew what color Wayne's casket would be. She said that as far as she knew, it would be a dark-colored wood. I felt relief, because I could then make the vision wrong, even though there was already the validation of his death. I still had that need to be wrong, though I didn't fully understand why.

Days later, we gathered at the mortuary in Plainview prior to the funeral at the Catholic church. I walked into the room, the tears welling up as my eyes scanned the room. Everything was exactly as it was in the vision I had been seeing, even the light silvery-blue casket.

I walked up to the casket and looked down. I saw Wayne's body dressed in the suit I had seen in the vision. I looked to the left, past the head of the casket, and viewed the single row of flowers I had seen in my mind's eye. To my right and beyond the foot of the casket was another single row of familiar flowers. I extended my right hand, placed it on his sleeve and, as I felt his arm, I heard him say, "It is okay, Susie Q." As the tears ran down my cheeks I thought, "Did I cause his death by seeing that vision?"

I reached into my pocket and pulled out a quarter, placing it in his right suit pocket. One of our standing jokes was that he would always place a quarter on the back of our toilet whenever he visited, as "payment" for the use of the facility. I never gave him one, so here it was. I heard him laugh and I felt that familiar embrace from the other side. For a fleeting moment, I wished I were there with him. Standing in the funeral home, reviewing scenes I had hidden so deeply and for so long, was one of the most painful moments of my life.

According to ancient Greek mythology, the dead need a coin to give the boatman who ferries them across the river Styx to the afterlife. At the time of Wayne's death, I didn't know that one of my prominent guides would be a Greek. I find it very interesting whenever events and information synchronize in this way. I don't believe it is just synchronicity, though. I believe that everything happens for a reason, though sometimes we can only see how and why in hindsight.

Wayne had made his final arrangements prior to his death. After the funeral formalities at the church, we went on to the cemetery. The pallbearers carrying my brother's body to the gravesite included Steven, my eldest son. As I observed my son, I thought quietly, "Is this when you finally feel grown up?" I heard a familiar, soft voice answer, "Only if that is what you choose." The voice was that of someone on the other side, and I realized that it was the voice I heard in my childhood and it was the voice from my vision that had asked, "Can you ignore this now?" In this moment, it shared with me that I could "choose."

I now see the person to whom this voice belongs as a monk wearing a brown robe with an attached hood that lies back on his shoulders, almost like a collar. He has beautiful, soft, brown eyes that glimmer with reflected light. He slightly resembles a cookie jar monk that I once saw in my childhood.

As my husband and I drove back to Minneapolis after the funeral and burial, I couldn't stop thinking about the events that led up to that day. I felt hurt, angry and resentful. I feared, childishly, that perhaps I had caused Wayne's death.

I felt a swell of anger because I felt cheated that I hadn't held out hope for his recovery as the others had. But, I could not believe in a hope that I didn't have. And I felt resentment as I thought, "How come I had to see that vision and then lose my brother?"

It would be hard for me to explain to my husband what was happening to me. He had always been a good listener and had been very supportive, but at the time, I had no idea how I could even start to share my feelings and experiences with him.

On May 1 the early wake-up calls started.

ONE EYE OPEN

"Wake up sleepy head, for your life is awaiting you!"

It was 4 a.m. and someone's gentle voice whispered in my ear, "Isn't it time to get up and take a shower?" I opened one eye and looked around; my husband was sleeping beside me and on the floor lays our Dalmatian, Josie. I shut my eyes and returned to sleep. Again, "Hey, isn't it time to take a shower?" I opened one eye and looked around. As I lay half asleep, I could hear the words repeating again.

I stumbled out of bed, deciding to get up and use the toilet. Sitting there, I got the urge to hop into the shower and start the day early. I returned to the bedroom to get my terry robe and my husband raised his head, asking, "What are you doing?" I quickly replied, "I can't sleep and I think I am going to take a shower."

As I stood in the shower, I heard my brother, and another familiar voice, greet me. I continued to shower. As I became more alert, I opened my eyes to the startling sight of Wayne and a man dressed in a brown robe standing in the shower with me. The feeling of pure and utter happiness rushed through me. It was the same feeling I had growing up when people from the other side popped in to visit or play with me.

I finally asked Wayne "What do you want?" I was so elated to see him and the Monk standing there, smiling. I quickly finished my shower and got dressed.

At the time, I didn't understand the connection between Wayne and the Monk who, as I got to know him, I would call Friar. They appeared very comfortable with each other, as if they were old and close friends.

I decided to go into our den and sit at my desk. Thoughts about what I had just seen were rushing through my head. I couldn't believe that the two of them had been just standing there, smiling. I had the feeling that there was more to their visit than what I could grasp. Suddenly, Wayne appeared by the door and walked across the room to where I was sitting. I heard his voice, "Morning, Susie Q." He then made a request. He asked me if I would call his wife, Marian, and let her know that *he was okay and that it is just like they talked about.* My first response to him was, "What do you mean?" He just smiled and stood there. He again asked me to please call Marian. I quickly replied "Wayne, I can't do that; she will think I am crazy!" I then replied, "Wayne, she's Catholic; you know I can't do that. Are you brain dead, too?"

My brother was asking me to call a devout Catholic woman whose husband just passed away and give her the message that her husband is okay and it is as they discussed. I truly did not want to do it. I remembered my brother in law John, and his reactions, and as far as I knew, the Catholic church in Plainview was much more rigid than the Lutheran.

I didn't want to meet a similarly hostile response. I also didn't want to cause Marian any pain.

He followed me around that morning for several hours, just smiling and staying in the background. I felt uncomfortable at the thought of calling his wife, but was happy to see him hanging out. I kept thinking about what he had asked me to do, but really felt that I would probably end up like a bug splattered on a windshield. No thank you!

I prepared my husband's breakfast and went to my desk. As I sat there, I thought that maybe I'd call my sister Bonnie and ask her what thoughts she had on this topic. She is older and I thought that maybe she'd be able to give me some good advice. I looked up her number in my address book and dialed the telephone. Not waiting for the person on the other end of the phone to say "Hello," I blurted out "Hi, Bonnie." Marian's familiar voice asked, "Susie?" I thought to myself, "Now, wait a minute. I dialed my sister's phone number. I know I did because I looked it up. How did I get Wayne's wife on the phone? It's not like I have their numbers memorized and confused them, and it's not like their phone numbers are on the same page. This is too weird."

I explained to Marian that I had dialed the wrong number but was happy to hear her voice. I felt almost tricked into having called her and, in truth, was not particularly happy about it. I asked her how she was doing and she replied she was doing okay but that it was hard to be without Wayne. I felt guided to ask her if she had ever heard of John Edward or watched *Crossing Over* on television. I thought if she did know him, I wouldn't feel so humiliated and I could maybe explain the situation. If she said no, she didn't know him, well, I thought that I wouldn't say anymore. She said, "Oh, yes. Wayne and I had been talking about John Edward and the possibilities of communicating after death the whole year prior to his passing." I took a deep breath and said, "Marian, Wayne is standing by me and wanted me to call you and let you know that it is just as you and he talked about." Marian's voice had a very surprised tone as she thanked me for the message. She said she had been hoping for some kind of sign. As we said goodbye, I could feel the sadness of her loss. I realized that the message does not really take the pain away, it just gives validation that love transcends death.

I hung up the phone. I was amazed that I survived the call and that Wayne was right. The confirmation was clear because of Marian's reaction. I hadn't known how she might react to Wayne's message. All I had known was that she was a very devout Catholic. She was raised in our small town and I would never have guessed that she and Wayne had those discussions.

When I look back on this, I often ask, "Why do organized religions view alternative expressions of spirituality with such foreboding?" It is a fair question. After all, the views and practices embraced by present-day religions don't necessarily reflect all or only the views of the spiritual masters and ideals that inspired those religions. Jesus did not form the Catholic or Lutheran Churches, nor did Buddha form the various systems of Buddhism.

I was raised Lutheran and still go to a Lutheran church. I believe in the Father, Son, and Holy Spirit, but I also do not deny that perhaps other masters, such as Buddha, walked the earth. Who knows what the "right" religion is, or if there is only one "right" religion? I find comfort and humor in the fact that I am a member of a Lutheran Church and my life guide is a Catholic monk. It definitely makes things interesting when one's guides are Native American or Tibetan or come from backgrounds different from one's own. In my view, this possibility sends the strong message that all spiritual views and practices are somehow connected, and it pleases me to know that, on the other side of the veil, religious divisions are not present.

Over the next few days, I continued to be greeted at 4 a.m. It seemed almost like a ritual. I would wake, hop into the shower and, before long, Wayne and the Monk would show up, sometimes accompanied by other relatives including Grandma, Grandpa, Dad, and Uncle Steve. It was getting kind of crowded in there. When the crowd began to swell to five people and more, I started feeling rather uncomfortable. They didn't seem to mind and, thank goodness, I'm not too modest, but a girl needs her privacy. She can get quite a reputation from taking a shower with that many people!

It was time to reclaim my shower for myself alone, but I didn't quite know how to accomplish that. On a morning when Wayne, the Monk, Grandma, Uncle Steve, and Dad were all in the shower with me, I finally just said, "Hey guys, you may not mind, but I am feeling uncomfortable with this. I promise I will try to listen when I am out of the bathroom, but this needs to slow down. After all, it is my bathroom!"

I soon learned that I could tune them all out if I concentrated on playing a small, electronic hand game of solitaire. I played while I was using the toilet—after all, the bathroom is a private space for private activities—and I only wished I could take it with me into the shower. Through experience, I have learned that spirits come into places like bathrooms because they reach out to us when and where we are the most receptive. When we are relaxed, we are in a receptive state. Whether it is in bed during the twilight hours as one awakens or in the bathroom shower or in the bath, they come through with messages to places where we are most open to receiving them.

Soon after my declaration in the shower, Christine and I talked about what was happening and I shared with her that it was getting to be a bit too much and that I felt out of control. We decided to go back to the bookstore and get some help. I bought John Edward's tapes entitled *Unleashing your Psychic Potential* and *Understanding your Angels and Meeting your Guides*.

My daughter became my confidant more than ever before. I shared my stories with her and she was very supportive. I was worried that if I told my husband about everything that was going on, he would have had me committed. And who would blame him? He saw me jump out of bed early every morning and he would come home from work and see me with headphones on, lying on my sofa. He would ask me what I was doing, and I would reply, "Meditating." He didn't question it, thank God.

Eventually, I started sharing bits and pieces of information with Jeff and, thank goodness, his reactions were quiet and supportive. Even though he had never dreamed of the changes that were occurring, he seemed willing to ride them out.

I found myself meditating three hours a day just to keep the voices out of my head. I was like an antenna turned on high power, receiving any message any spirit wanted to send. I was a reluctant medium to say the least, and at this point I wanted to find a way to stop seeing and hearing them. I was still angry about seeing my brother's death, and I developed a stubborn attitude because I was fighting back the pain of it all. I had not found a valid reason for being selected to have and use these special abilities. My life was changing and I felt I wanted to control those changes.

In one of our conversations, Christine mentioned to me that John Edward had included a referral list on the back of his book. We looked and found several names. Christie decided to call Lydia Clar and when I saw Sandy Anastasi's name, heard Wayne say, "Remember, John in his book states that she was his only psychic development teacher." I decided to try Sandy and thought, if she can teach psychic development, then perhaps she can help me find a way to shut off the visits and voices.

I dialed the number listed for Sandy Anastasi, and a woman answered the phone. When I asked for Sandy, she replied, "I'm Sandy." At that moment, I felt instant relief mixed with excitement. I told my story to Sandy and said, "Sandy, I am not psychic; I just see and hear dead people." Sandy quickly replied, "Susan, if you see and hear dead people, you are psychic, but not all psychics see or hear dead people."

I asked her if there was a way she could teach me to shut this off. She replied that she could, if that was what I chose, but that I should come to Florida and see her. Perhaps, she suggested, I could take some of her classes. For the first time, I felt a huge weight lifted off my shoulders and with it, the feeling of relief descended.

I then said, "Sandy, what a coincidence that I actually got you live on the phone!" She was quick to reply, "You think so. By the way, I never answer this phone." OOPS! I hoped that I hadn't insulted her by suggesting that our phone conversation was the result of mere coincidence. Her next series of classes were scheduled to start in June and I agreed that I would be there.

She then suggested that I receive a reading from one of her teachers, Jason Oliver. She said he was very good and I could call back if I decided to have a reading with him.

Sandy also mentioned a hotel where I might stay that was within walking distance to her classroom and was reasonably priced. I immediately heard Wayne say, "No, stay at the

Holiday Inn." I asked Sandy if there was a Holiday Inn around there and she said that there was, and that it was located across the river. She also said that the hotel would be too far to walk to and from.

I shared this information with my husband and he was very supportive about my taking a trip to Florida, if that was what I wanted. My daughter wanted to go with me, but with her three little ones, it would be difficult for her to get away. We talked about us taking another class together at a later time.

I called and made a reservation at the Holiday Inn. The information that I received from Wayne before had been correct and I decided I would take a "leap of faith" and trust in the information I was given. I had never been to the west coast of Florida.

I was so excited about going to Florida and meeting Sandy that I hoped the trip would begin the next day. I felt relief knowing that I could get some help with what was happening.

My brother Jon and my sister Bonnie were not opposed to my taking the trip to see Sandy. They actually supported the idea. My other siblings were less than receptive to the idea. It seems that caretaking and dictating one's views to others is a "birthright" in my family. Making others wrong so that one can feel right is also a family trait. And the females in my family have never been shy or soft-spoken. All the things I was experiencing elicited a lot of uninvited, unwanted commentary from the female members my family. Though I know that they reacted with the best of intentions, I found their reactions difficult to bear.

When I announced that I was moving forward in search of an answer to why I was "seeing" visions and dead people,

I received an email from my sister Nancy. She copied the email to the whole family, including Wayne's wife. Nancy strongly implied that I was more or less taking the family to the "Devil" if I pursued the answers to my questions. Needless to say, it made great conversation between them, often at my expense.

It got so out of hand that, while my mother was in the hospital, my brother-in-law John and my sister Nancy felt that I shouldn't visit and spend time with her. They thought that I might cause harm to her were she to pass while I was there.

One day, I was waiting for the hospital elevator. After it arrived and the doors opened, Nancy and John got off, walking way around me as if I had the plague. I remember thinking how childish this behavior was. But of course, Friar and Wayne were there to help me through these kinds of trials.

I was taking blind leaps of faith. Wayne's and Friar's gentle voices were the encouragement that I needed. Their strength carried me further than I could have gone on my own. Wayne's love helped fill the voids that I felt growing between my family and me. Wayne's and Friar's laughter was the music that I listened to in the still moments when I felt doubt about myself.

I cannot stress enough how important the presence and support of my daughter, Christine, was to me during this time. It was Christie's encouragement and experiences that helped me make sense of all that was happening. Furthermore, because of her psychic abilities or clairsenses, she was attuned to Wayne as well. Both of us were and are able to see Wayne, to feel and hear him, as we can with each of our guides and with many others on the other side.

Just weeks after we first made those phone calls to John Edward's referrals, Christie and I began to have four way conversations that included, in addition to the both of us, her life guide, Charlie, and mine, Friar. It then became clear to us that we were never alone and we had something profound in common.

Whether we are together or apart, both of us can talk with each other's guides, as well as with our relatives and others who are beyond the veil. Today, traveling across the states in her car or even just across town is fun, since when we start up a discussion about any topic, both of our guides often chime in. One of the funniest times we've had in such a situation was when we had just done a group reading and Charlie and Friar starting shuffling their feet and singing the song, "My Girl."

Christie is as instrumental in my moving through this journey as Wayne and my guides are. She is able to bring balance to problems and discussions, especially when decisions need to be made. Her psychic foresight has been validated by my journey. She KNEW so much about me and had much more faith in me than I did. Her presence in the physical world helped me to establish the strong link I have between the physical and the elusive world beyond the veil.

The past years have been a time of change for my whole family, not just for me. When I reflect back, it seems bizarre that members of my family would fight amongst themselves about my desire to understand what I was experiencing. Three years have passed since my brother's death and my family still struggles to meet my experiences with understanding, though they do show more tolerance. For most of the members of my family, this book, if they choose to read it, will give them the first true insight into what my experiences have really meant to me. My family's resistance has taught me that one cannot change what one doesn't want to change. I can only be the example of the change.

from the SHOWER *to* NEW ORLEANS

"Just because something is over the horizon
does not make it nonexistent; it merely means that it is
within reach through a leap of faith."

An almost steady stream of conversation was coming through from the other side. It now happened not only at 4 a.m., but off and on throughout the day. It seemed like the flood gates had been removed and I was really in my element. But being bombarded with all of these voices and information was making it increasingly difficult to do much else. It seemed as if they were walking me through life holding my hand, and that I was in school every waking hour, learning about the connections between this side and the other.

It was as if I was on a different mission every day, and they were there to teach me how to trust the information they were giving me and do what needed to be done. And everything they taught me was validated. Christie and I were building a connection with the other side both separately and together. In fact, what we learned during this time became the basis for the curriculum of our ever-evolving educational programs. All that we did and learned during this time strengthened the bonds we had with each other and the bonds we were developing with other side.

Listening to and working with John Edward's tapes became an essential part of each day for me personally. The information on them was helpful and the meditations were the only thing that helped me shut out the voices. I found that I needed periods of silence every day, that only through silence could I stay present to myself.

In fact, I knew that I needed something in addition to the words spinning around me at such a fast pace. I discovered that the missing part was having a sense of myself in the midst of outside influences. I found myself in the stillness of meditation.

I was becoming increasingly comfortable with my connection with the other side and I had no feelings of fear or negativity from the visits. But they became so frequent that I felt like I was in "psychic school" 24/7. I still had an underlying concern about what I had experienced in Rochester with my brother in law, in particular with John's "ghost stories." It had planted a seed of doubt in me that was still there.

I started using Mr. Edward's instructions about self-protection on a regular basis. His tapes helped me turn my shower into a place where I felt more secure. Wayne, my grandmother and the Monk were the only ones who could get through to me in the shower. I started feeling like maybe there was hope in being able to shut out or control the voices and visitations.

One of his tapes had a section on meeting your guides. Working with the tape, I discovered that the Monk was my life guide. I had seen him in the past but did not know what his appearance meant or what his purpose was. I now understand his role and welcome his unique, humor-filled presence. When Wayne and Friar would laugh, I could see both their bellies shaking from the laughter. I have seen everything from the very serious to the humorous side of Wayne, and a special gentleness is always present with Friar. And, although I am now aware of the thirty-six guides that help me and work with me, Friar is the one to whom I feel closest.

The early morning, 4 a.m. wake-up calls continued. One morning, I heard Friar's gentle voice ask, "Are you ready to get up?" By now, I looked forward to the morning wake-up call and usually ran into the shower. This day was no different, at least not yet. This time, when I got into the shower, I heard what sounded like Wayne playing music; the sound had his trademark "twirls" or cascading notes in it and it sounded like a choir of angels was singing. I first heard the words "Wash All My Cares Away" and the word "refrain." The music kept playing over and over and it became louder and clearer. I ran dripping wet from the shower to grab a piece of paper and pencil. I ran back into the shower to start writing the words down so I wouldn't forget them. The melody was clear and the words, "Wash All My Cares Away," along with other words, kept coming through. It seemed as if angels were singing; tears rolled down my face as I heard Wayne leading the song. It was simply beautiful.

I didn't know what to do with the words and melody I had heard. My understanding, though, gradually evolved. I saw a picture of Wayne and his wife and heard that it would help if I called Bonnie, my sister who lived in Preston, Minnesota. I remembered that she knew how to compose music: perhaps she could help make the words and melody into a real song. With excitement, I ran for a robe and called Bonnie. When she answered the phone, I told her that I had been in the shower when a beautiful melody and accompanying words started coming through. The song had played over and over. I told her that I needed help, since I could not write music. I shared with her that I was sure it was Wayne who had been playing the melody, because I could hear his trademark twirls in it.

She mentioned that she felt it was a confirmation for her, because no one ever acknowledged she wrote music except Wayne. She felt that the song was coming through for her. In retrospect, I can honestly state that it was bigger than that, but I didn't understand it all at the time. I worked with her for some time over the phone. I would try to sing what I heard as the refrain and to give her as many of the words as I had been able to write down in the shower. I heard Wayne request that I bring the finished song to Marian. I asked Bonnie to please help. She felt she could work on it and promised to get back to me so that I could hear it and see if what she wrote was just what I had heard earlier that morning and fill in the missing notes and words to complete the song. Bonnie said she would take it and play it for Marian, just as Wayne had requested.

Bonnie worked very hard on the song and took it to Wayne's wife. Because of my trips to Florida, Bonnie and I were unable to get together during that summer. Bonnie, excited about the song, copied it to disc and let some relatives hear it while she was in Oregon at a family gathering.

I was upset with her when I found this out. I felt that, out of fairness, she should have sent the recording to me to hear first before she shared it with other family member. But I understand how enthusiastic she felt.

I first heard Bonnie's recording when she sent the disc to me that December, just before my birthday. I couldn't hold back the tears as I listened for the first time to the physical world version of the song. Bonnie had done a wonderful job. When I later met with Marian, she showed me a letter Wayne had written her, promising her a song. It was dated Christmas 2001, and read:

MY PROMISE
THIS IS MY PROMISE TO DO MY BEST TO RECORD
A NEW TAPE FOR YOU.
MERRY CHRISTMAS MARIAN, Love you much.
WAYNE

She commented how beautiful she thought the song was. There it was, and what a huge validation.

Many times when people from the other side send information through, the messages have more than one meaning. In this particular case, Wayne's message was the fulfillment of a promise, a gift he was sending to his wife. But the message was more than that. Wayne's message for Bonnie, since I had to ask for her help arranging and adding to the song, was an enormous witness to Bonnie's musical side, a validation that made her heart sing. And for me, well… I think it would be difficult to replicate, let alone describe, the feeling of elation I felt that day in the shower when I heard the beauty of the instruments and the voices of the choir of angels that made up that song.

When I look back at the fact that I felt I had to return to the shower in order to finish transcribing the song, I find it amusing. I really trusted the shower to be the place for communication, but I could have simply sat at my desk and finished writing down the song. It's interesting how our perceptions change as we change.

As great and as difficult as the experience was for Bonnie and me, we both have no doubt that Wayne came through loud and clear! In retrospect, we recognize the way it brought us understanding of the ways the other side can touch our lives, how love transcends death, and how valuable such experiences are.

Later that spring, and with Mother's Day fast approaching, Christine scheduled an astrology reading and gave it to me as a gift. I thought it was a waste of money because, despite my own experiences with the other side, I didn't believe in that "woo woo" stuff. I thanked her for the thought and, after some discussion, I decided to go along with her plan. At least it would be entertaining and we'd get to spend time together. Christine explained that this woman had given her readings before and that she was fantastic. Now go figure: I am hearing from dead relatives and acknowledge that as "normal," but think that a reading is what? Woo woo?

"Okay, what do you do at a reading?" I asked my daughter. She replied, "You just sit back and listen." When the day of the appointment arrived, I knocked on the door and a pleasant woman named Pat answered, welcoming us and offering us cups of tea. "No thank you, I have never learned to drink that stuff," I replied.

There were no candles, no potions, and, feeling a little more at ease I guess, I decided I could handle this. She explained that she looked at my "chart" in order to do my reading. At the time, I had no idea what she was talking about.

After studying my astrological chart, she named the exact years of my children's births. She talked about events that had taken place in my life, and everything she said was right on.

"Lucky guesses?" I wondered to myself. She then noted that she saw me writing a book and I thought, "She is drinking too much green tea." I never had any intention of writing anything. Then she mentioned seeing at least three books. And then she said, "I see you on a stage doing this work."

Okay. When she spoke about my mother, she was 100 percent accurate. The information about my family was also 100 percent accurate. But what was all this other stuff? She also mentioned that I would become a bit eccentric and said she saw me with tarot cards. After it was all over, I told my daughter it had been fun, but that I thought it was a little far off.

In retrospect, I owe Pat a huge apology and, though she did say that she wasn't psychic herself, I believe that Pat uses her psychic abilities, and not just her talent of reading charts, very well. She was right about every thing she said that day. Since that reading, I've written books and I do readings for groups, clubs, and events nationwide. Christie and I have had a show at the huge Northrup Auditorium on the University of Minnesota campus, and I teach psychic development classes. And yes, I do use tarot cards.

After my Mother's Day reading with Pat, Christine shared with me that she had tarot cards; I mentioned that they really scared me. In my mind, they were for witches and goblins or whom- and whatever. And anyway, when we went to the bookstore, I could not find any deck that looked like something I wanted to try.

As I reflect back at my reactions to the Rider Tarot Deck, which is one of the most common decks of tarot cards, and the illustrations on its individual cards, I understand why I felt that way. As a medium, I am drawn to less rigid, more abstract images.

Tarot cards are only one of the many tools a psychic can use in a reading and a psychic using them as an aid is a very common and widely accepted practice. Tarot card spreads can resemble the Jewish Kabbalah's figure of the Tree of Life, and the meaning of individual cards is based on Kabbalistic principles. Studying the meaning of the spreads and cards can give a psychic direction in her readings. In the deck, for example, there is a "Death" card. This card made me very uncomfortable when I first, saw it, but when I learned that it represents change or the severity of a change (or no change, if it appears upside down in a spread), it isn't literally "Death." It was out of ignorance that I ran like the wind from any deck of tarot in those days. I have since learned the proper value of these cards.

But that spring, I was still ignorant and suspicious. Late one morning, while I was standing in the shower, I got the sudden urge to jump out, put on clothes, get in my car, and drive to a particular metaphysical store, Present Moment, located in south Minneapolis, on Grand Avenue. So I hopped out of the shower, dried off, got dressed, and left with my hair still damp. I drove to the store, walked in, and looked across the room: there were all kinds of tarot decks. I thought, "What would I want to be here for?" I heard, "Look down." When I looked down, I saw a book titled *Tarot of the Spirit*. I picked it up and, as I glanced back up at the shelves, I saw the matching deck. I bought them and immediately returned home.

I called Christine to share with her my "mission" for that day. It included the trip, the purchase of a deck of tarot cards, and a book on how to use them. Hearing my news, she was very surprised. Later, she ended up purchasing the same deck. This particular deck is more abstract for me than many others, and doesn't look archaic or scary! It has become a deck that, along with another, I use regularly.

Soon after my purchase, I bought two tickets for John Edward's June 6, 2002, show in New Orleans. I thought getting away would be a perfect birthday gift for Christie and would give both of us a special time to be alone. We hadn't gotten away together since she'd had her children. We were very excited about having a few days away together and seeing Mr. Edward do his work live on stage. In fact, I was so excited that I broke out in hives. On some level I must have had some awareness or anticipation of what was to happen.

My daughter and I arrived in New Orleans excited just to be there and to watch John work in person. I had made reservations at the Hilton Garden Inn, on Lake Pontchartrain. The show was at the Convention Center, which the people at the hotel said would be right next door.

Christine was hoping to bring a message home for someone, but we worked hard to keep our expectations to a quiet roar. The auditorium was full. I was astonished at how far people had come and how many people had gathered to see him. I had no idea how popular he was.

As we watched John come out on the stage, I could feel the energy in the room rise: each person desperately hoped to be one of the group of people selected to receive a reading. The feeling of the anticipation from the lady in front of me who was hoping to hear from her dead son; the excitement of the woman behind me who brought her whole family, hoping to hear from her mother; the yearning of a young woman three rows forward who carried a picture of her baby who died of SIDS. The range of emotion seemed endless.

I felt like I was a sardine in a can with 2,000 other sardines. It felt uncomfortable. In fact, it was overwhelming to see all these people waiting to hear a message meant just for them, and I wondered how John would be able to give all of them what they came for.

John Edward told us that attending his show was like coming to a birthday party. He used the analogy to let the audience members know that he'd give a reading to some of them, but not to all. He used the analogy of a birthday party. He said that the people who'd be getting the "gift" of the reading would be like those whose birthday the party was celebrating. Though only a few would get gifts, everyone attending would get "a piece of the cake" by witnessing the readings and sharing in those moments.

John was genuine and his use of the analogy showed his concern. He did quite a few readings, but there were over 2000 people in attendance. Mr. Edward read approximately ten to fifteen people that night, and had a question-and-answer session. During the show, he moved from one side of the auditorium to other and into the balcony areas as he randomly picked people from the audience. He displayed a great sense of humor when working with his audience, and even when a reading was difficult, he moved through it like a master of his art.

I discovered during this show that knowing death does not stop the connection we have with people who have passed away. That message was incredibly important to each person sitting in that auditorium. I had not really known of people's need to connect with loved ones, nor did I know how many people have this need. It took me by complete surprise. Since I had always felt connected to those on the other side, I never felt such a yearning. Attending John's show opened my eyes to what it must be like not to see or hear people who have passed on.

And even though my reason for attending was to see John Edward do his work, I felt the heaviness in the hearts of each person who had hoped that his or her relative would be the one that John would listen to and connect them with.

And so, as the show came to an end, I felt the disappointments of so many people who had come so far but who did not get a reading. Tears ran down my face as we left the auditorium. I felt like I was grieving for everyone who was leaving. I commented to Christie that it hadn't felt like any birthday party I had ever attended! And then I looked at her and told her that I would share with these people what I see, if they would be interested in listening. "But," I thought, "who am I?" Despite my initial doubt, in that decisive moment I found a reason to stop fighting what was happening to me and to choose to do the work of a psychic medium. I found a purpose for my gifts and a passion for the work!

Christine and I talked about how amazing it would be to work with John Edward, or to be able to give a reading to those people seeking one. Our excitement actually wasn't about Mr. Edward personally, but about what he stood for. I had never been to a place where so many grieving people hoped to hear from their loved ones. It was emotionally moving for me to see that.

I was tired and wanted to return to our room, so I decided to retire early. I had so many feelings running through me: the hope Christine had for a reading and her disappointment; the feeling of others not receiving the reading they hoped for; and for the first time, a feeling that I might be able to help someone by what I could do.

Christine had decided to go down to the hot tub. It was getting late when Christine rushed back into the room, excited. "Mom," she exclaimed, "you have to come down to the pool, now." Her eyes gleaming and excited, she told me that she had met someone down at the pool and stressed that I "needed to come down there, now." Reluctantly, and with a bit of grumbling, I went with her to the pool.

There, sitting by the pool, was a dark-haired woman and a young man. My daughter introduced the woman as April, mentioning that she was from Texas. April had come to the show with her nephew, Adam, to see John work and with the hope of receiving a reading that would bring in her deceased husband.

We struck up a conversation as if we were old friends. April said that she had lost her husband in February, at the age of fifty-one. I could see Eric sitting beside her and his twenty-two-year-old nephew. I noticed that Adam resembled Eric almost immediately. Adam had come along with April to keep her company. I don't think he shared her interest in psychic phenomena, but he was open to the possibilities. He sure looked a lot like Eric.

April shared a story about a trip she had taken to New York to attend one of John Edward's seminars. I remember thinking, "How fortunate she was to spend a day learning from Mr. Edward." I remember her telling us about a psychic, Robert Brown, who was at John Edward's seminar.

That evening, April did a short reading for Christie by placing a piece of family jewelry that Christie had brought along for the weekend between her hands. It was interesting to see April hold it and hear her describe a church and some other scenes that Christie later confirmed were about her husband's father, who died when her husband was young. The church April described was the church Joe's dad and mom were married in.

The conversation went on well into the night. April talked about the seminar, her family, what it was like living in Texas, and, of course, the loss of husband.

I sensed that April carried sadness about her loss with her, and it felt very similar to the grief I felt around people in the auditorium earlier that night. For some reason, April and I gravitated toward each other and we ended up talking into the wee hours of the morning.

I explained that I was planning on going to Florida in a couple of weeks to take a class with Sandy Anastasi. I invited April along. April loved the idea, saying that she would be happy to go along with me. We agreed that we would make arrangements to share a hotel room and car.

It felt as if we were old friends, that I had known her forever. I was so happy to have her join me on the trip to Florida. April and I talked almost every day after I arrived back home. It was nice to have one more person share in what was happening.

the MESSAGE *from* JASON

*"Validations are food for our feeling of worthiness,
and the fuel that can help drive us."*

One day, just prior to my leaving for my trip to Florida, I
awoke excited. I was going to get a reading over the phone by
Jason Oliver. Jason was a medium and a mediumship teacher
at Starchild, Sandy's school. Jason also worked with Disney
World on many occasions as the "Grand Wizard" and did
readings for parties that Disney had. Sandy said he was really
good and I was hoping to get answers about my dad. The
conversation with my brother-in-law had played over and
over in my head. I felt that if a medium like Jason—someone
else who saw "dead people"—could validate my own experience of my father, I'd know if what I saw about him revealed
the truth. Speaking with Jason could help me close that
chapter. At that point in my life, I really wanted and needed
someone else's description of my dad.

To prepare myself for my reading, I decided to burn some moxa. My daughter had introduced me to moxa. It looked similar to a paper-covered cigar. It even had something that looked like tobacco in it. She said, "Mom, burning this just before your reading will help raise and balance your energy." She also said something about my "ch'i," but back then I didn't know ch'i from tea! The moxa stick appeared to be some kind of dried herbs wrapped in paper: when you light it, it smolders and has a very strong and weird smell! But I trusted her about this. As the time for my reading approached, I meditated and got comfortable in my living room, waiting for the time to call him. I lit the moxa stick and sat in great anticipation. The clock turned to the magic time and I called Starchild. The receptionist was quick to inform me that I had missed the reading. They were on Eastern Standard Time and I was on Central. I could not believe that I didn't take that into account. I asked if I could leave him a message. I learned that his schedule was full but I left a message indicating that if something opened up, to please call me, I would be waiting. I hung up and felt extremely disappointed that I had messed up this moment. I was sitting on my sofa when the phone rang. The voice on the other end said, "Jason would like you to call him right away."

I dialed Jason's direct number and he answered. He explained that he could not connect with his client, so he asked her to reschedule. He went on to say that this had not happened to him before. In my head, I said "Thank you, Wayne and Friar."

As Jason started the reading, he brought in my grandmother and relayed lots of information about my family. He also asked me what I had been doing prior to the reading, because he felt like I was flying or had had twelve pots of coffee. I explained that I had burned a moxa stick and he said,

"I think you are supposed to burn just a little of it, not the whole thing." OOPS! He then said the words, "Your brother wants me to ask, (and he used the exact words) what it was that struck terror in your heart." I could not believe my ears. I explained the story of my brother-in-law, how he felt about my dad, and how I felt. Jason went to my dad and gave validations (information I could validate about my dad) and then said, "Honey, it is just as you see it; your brother-in-law works from fear and that brings with it other things. It is not your dad bringing it in." I felt immense relief to have that confirmation. I am still grateful to Jason for that moment.

The reading with Jason was a huge validation for me. It lifted me up enough to see that I saw something of what he saw. I began to get a sense of what really resonated with me, what my truth was! This experience allowed me to take the steps away from my brother-in-law's religious dogma and see the beauty in living and acting in faith rather than fear.

I felt like chains were removed from around my ankles and I was free to take flight! I was exhilarated that, for the first time in my life, a complete stranger who worked in the spirit communication field validated my "visions." It brought witness to my life!

It was early morning on Father's Day, 2002. I called my daughter and shared with her that, in celebration of Jason's reading and my pending trip to Florida, I would like to go out to Fort Snelling National Cemetery and honor my family by putting single white roses on my dad's, grandfather's, and grandmother's graves. She said she was going to put one on her father-in-law's grave as well, and she would drive over with the kids to pick me up.

We stopped at a grocery store to pick up the flowers. I ran in to get them and, as I approached the flower section of the store, I heard a song. The song was "The Yellow Rose of

Texas." I had been hearing things from the other side so much that it didn't surprise me. I entered the Flower Department. My intention was to buy four roses, one rose for each of grave. As I searched the selection for the four white roses, I heard Wayne say, "Susie, you need six." I responded with my familiar question. "Why?" I replied. "I need four." And then I heard him and the monk in the brown robe say, "It looks like you may need six." Well, instead of having the discussion with them in the middle of the store, I picked up the six flowers and said "Fine."

Next, I heard Wayne say, "Don't forget the yellow rose." Again I thought, "Why?" but just picked up the yellow rose and decided to buy that one, too. The music was still playing in my head.

Seeing me walking out to the car, my daughter took one look and asked, "Now what? Why are there so many?" I replied, "Just drive. I'll explain on the way."

Such surprises were becoming a daily occurrence and we started relaxing more as we began accepting them.

Fort Snelling National Cemetery is located in Bloomington, Minnesota, near I-494 and the 34th Avenue exit. As we drove down I-494, I was explaining to her what I had heard. She couldn't think of any more than four graves and didn't understand why we needed six white plus one yellow rose, either. All of a sudden, Christine turned to go across the Minnesota River on Cedar Avenue. I asked her why she was heading that way. She replied, "I don't know." It was then I realized she was headed toward my Mother's home. We both thought, "Hey, wait a minute, something must be at work."

She turned the car around and I asked "the other side" to just please stop. I would consideer going out to Mother's after the cemetery, but it was getting to be mid-afternoon and we were worried about what time the cemetery would be closing.

A light misting rain was falling as we arrived at Fort Snelling Cemetery. Christine parked by the building where on a computer visitors can look up gravesite locations. As I got out of the car to go into the building, I noticed the air started to change. It felt like it was about to rain.

I ran into the building and stood in line. I approached the locator computer and punched in each of the four names. As I completed my task, I heard "Well, what about David and the baby?" Oh my goodness; I had forgotten about them. There were now six. I was so excited as I hurried to the car. I got in and exclaimed, "Christine, they were right again. You won't believe this, but there are six! I forgot my sister's baby and her ex-husband."

We delivered flowers to the graves, beginning with my Grandma and Grandpa. We decided to do them in order of location and would end up at my father's grave. It went very well, until we got to his. The grave is located toward the back of the cemetery and as we started to look for his, it seemed like they weren't in order. Closing time was quickly approaching and visitors would have to leave in only ten minutes. The rain started and we kept looking, but to no avail. Tearfully, I finally asked, "Hey guys, I have listened to you and not asked for anything. Please help me find Dad's grave. It is very important to me and I need help."

I heard the man in the brown robe say, "Look for the grave toward the back row with the red flower stuck in the ground." I yelled to Christine, "Christine, look for the grave with a red flower." She replied, "Mom, there is a grave here with three red flowers" Again I shouted, "Christine, look for the grave with only one red flower!" As I shouted that message, I looked up to the left and saw a grave with one red flower stuck in the ground. It was my dad's grave. My heart filled with gratitude.

As I stood in front of his grave, I could feel a group from the other side stand alongside me. I was elated that I could place the flower there that day and, for the first time as an adult, I felt the comfort and loving grace that surrounded me when I was a child. I felt the comfort of knowing that the people I loved were there and had helped me, and that I could ask them for help. It was as if I were frozen for a moment in time.

As we returned to the car, I asked Christine if she would be willing to drive out to my mother's place. We agreed that time was getting really tight, but we would go.

On the way out there, I kept asking what I was supposed to say to her when I got there. I received no verbal response, but could sense a smile and hear the word "patience." Now, that word was starting to really drive me nuts. I was tired of having patience, but I would venture to speculate that they were hoping to help create a better dialogue between us, or to build a stronger "telephone line" between this world and theirs. It is also clear to me now that their time line is not ours, and what we feel is important at a particular moment, may be seen quite differently from their perspective.

My mother was not aware that we were coming to visit, and what, I asked my guides, could I possibly say to her when I knocked on her door and handed her the yellow rose? Guess what? They just smiled.

It was about a twenty minute drive to her home in Eagan, Minnesota. When we arrived, Christine said, "Hey, I'll stay in the car with the kids, Mom." I tried to encourage her to come in, but she refused. I was on my own on this one.

As I walked up the walk, I saw Wayne and the man in the brown robe smile. I thought to myself, "If I get shot down by this, I may choose never to talk to them again!" I was not particularly pleased about knocking on her door and having absolutely no clue about what to say. They were silent.

At the time, my mother was feeling overwhelmed by her son's death and had a tendency to be rather negative. Mother had never been shy about stating her opinion. It sometimes would come out a bit rough around the edges, and more so lately due to Wayne's death and her loneliness. Characteristically, I would stay away from her when she was in a negative mood. I always took that type of thing very personally.

As she opened the door, Mom said, "What are you doing here? You usually call." I replied, "Christine and I were out driving and I thought I would drop in." Now this is really out of character, because my mother likes visitors to phone in advance. She lives alone and does not open her door unless she knows who is there! We went up the stairs to her kitchen, I kept the yellow rose hidden behind my back, just like a child. I placed it with my purse on the chair so that it would be out of sight. At this point, I felt clueless and wondered what I had gotten myself into now!

She offered me the usual soda and asked, "Why isn't Christine coming in?" I mentioned that we had been out at the cemetery and that we both had to get back home. Mom said that she wished we had come out earlier so that we could have stayed longer. Since Dad's death in 1989, she had been living alone and looked forward to people visiting. I jumped up out of the chair, as the other side kept prodding me about presenting the rose. "Mom, I was at the grocery store, and the song "The Yellow Rose of Texas" kept playing in my head. I heard Wayne asking me to buy this rose," I told her, as I picked the flower up. I continued, "I have no clue what the message is, but I know this is for you. Perhaps he is just saying "Hi" and letting you know that he loves you. I don't know."

Mom looked a little puzzled but got up and put the flower into a vase with water. I explained, "Mom, I have to get going." I left as fast as I could. When I got to the car, Christine was laughing. She said I didn't look happy and asked what had happened. I told her what had happened and that I was really disappointed that they didn't help me more.

We chit-chatted all the way back to my house. She dropped me off and had to leave right away. Jeff was home and I explained to him what had happen. He smiled as he always does and just listened. I don't think he knew what to say or how to react to the things I was sharing with him.

That evening around 7 p.m., the phone rang. Jeff answered the phone and called, "Sue, the phone is for you!" As I came over to take the receiver, he added, "Sue, it's your mom and she seems to be laughing." To my recollection, my mom has never called laughing. I answered the phone by saying, "Mom?" She exclaimed, "I had to call you. Sue, you are so wrong! Wayne hated the "Yellow Rose of Texas!" When he was stationed in Texas while in the Air Force, he had come home on leave. Your sister learned to play that song on the piano for his homecoming. When he arrived and she was playing it, Wayne grabbed my arm and took me to the kitchen. He told me that he was so sick of that song, because that was all he had heard while he was there." She apologized but thought she should let me know that my interpretation was wrong.

As we hung up the phone, I had to smile. My mother had no clue what I was going through, but her response was a validation that she had received a message from Wayne! My sister was ten years my senior. I must have been five or so at the time he came home on leave. I would like to believe that guidance was teaching me to have patience, trust, and some faith mixed in. I still smile to think that it made my mom laugh, and that she didn't question it any further. After all, she didn't know I was talking to dead people. Or did she? She was missing him so much, and to think that it made her smile…. My heart felt like it would leap out of my chest from happiness.

It was still June and Christie and I decided to take a trip to Plainview to see Wayne's wife. We decided to drive to Plainview in Christie's car, and as we were driving out of Rochester, Christie suddenly took a right-hand turn onto an unfamiliar road. Rochester is about thirty miles from Plainview and neither of us had a map or knew any routes except the main one. As Christie veered off the highway onto a country road, I asked her where she thought she was going, and she said she had no idea. By this time, I just sat back.

We laughed and just had fun driving through the countryside. We went through rural areas with beautiful scenery. The rolling hills and green pastures were a welcome site. We laughed at my dad's story about how black-and-white cows give white milk and brown and white cows give chocolate milk. We listened to a cassette of Wayne's organ music. The sky was beautifully blue with soft, wispy, white clouds that resembled cotton. Our thoughts were not on the direction we were heading and we just treated it as a wonderful drive through the country. We arrived in Plainview five minutes ahead of schedule, and came into the town right by the Cemetery where Wayne is buried. We drove right through downtown and up to Wayne's house. We both just smiled and enjoyed the ride.

Messages and events were happening quite regularly and we were learning to just go with it all. Synchronicities were getting to be common-place events and it was almost as if the other side was working with us to build that unshakable trust that we'd need so that we could take "leaps of faith" when they were necessary.

We were in "school" seven days a week and loved it. In fact, I felt like a part of me was finally coming out to play. Even today, when I am working I still feel like I am playing, in part because my work is the song that sings in my heart.

It is interesting that I can remember my mother telling me stories of sightings she had seen when I was a child. But for a number of years now she doesn't seem to want to talk about anything that connects the two sides. I hope someday to know why and I plan on asking her. Recently, though, she has moved to an assisted living home, and on one of my visits she told me, "I had a dream about Dolly, next door. She said she would be leaving and I shouldn't worry about her, but she would not be here anymore." She then mentioned that Dolly was found dead the next morning. It is interesting to see her acknowledge her foresight in a way, and yet she prefers to see it merely as a dream and not as a visit.

The other side has a way of coming through, even when we are in the twilight of our sleep, and I am sure that Dolly found that opening when she visited my mother. I found it interesting that it didn't seem to bother my mom and that she treated it as a mere coincidence. Of course, when two things become a "co" "incidence," I believe it is two things coming together to cause an event. And, bless my Mom. She received the wonderful message that she didn't have to worry about her neighbor.

When I now teach students or give a lecture, one of the first questions that usually arise is, "How do we know if it is a visit or a dream?" I generally explain that people from the other side visit us regularly, but we do not always hear or see them. It is usually easiest for them to get through in a place where we are most relaxed or feel most private. These places are generally in our twilight state just before awakening in the morning or in the bathroom. Generally the difference between a dream and a visit is that a dream tends to fade from our memories as we wake and go about our days while a visit will become stronger in our memory during the day.

June, 2002 I continued to prepare for my trip to Florida and the day of my departure finally arrived! My husband drove me to the airport. I felt Jeff's concern for me and the support he was giving, and knew that he would be there for me in this journey. He was like a rock on the shoreline where I could sit and look out over the vastness of the ocean waves. I felt how truly blessed I was to have found him after so many years.

At that moment, I couldn't help but think that, if I were still married to my ex-husband, I would not be sitting in a car, being driven to the airport on my way to meet psychics, and probably would not have been supported on my quest on any level. I believe now that my marrying Jeff and embracing my gifts was part of divine timing.

I had known Jeff when I was young and had reconnected with him when my fourteen year marriage ended in 1986. During my marriage, I had found myself thinking of Jeff many times and wondered what ever happened to him. One night years ago, Christine and I were just hanging out together. I shared with her that I was thinking of this man and we got into a discussion about whether I should look him up. Christine encouraged me to make that phone call. I was actually a bit scared to do it, and yet inside I knew how badly I wanted to connect with him. I looked up his phone number but wasn't sure if I should call.

"What happens if he is married?" I had thought. I didn't want to get a wife on the phone! I then looked up his parents' phone number and was surprised to find that it hadn't changed in all those years. I just left my name and phone number and figured that Jeff would either call and I would be in shock or he wouldn't. That same evening, the phone rang and it was him. My heart just leapt when I heard his voice. I couldn't believe that after all these years I was having a conversation with Jeff. I was amazed that not only was I now listening to his voice, but that we were actually going to get together. All I could think was, "Oh my goodness! I have had three kids, and am how many years older?"

How can a woman look pounds lighter and younger in twenty-four hours? I was so nervous about meeting Jeff that I made arrangements to meet him at a roller rink while my children were skating. I remember how amazing it was that, when he walked through the door that night, it was as if time was standing still. That night years ago was wonderful.

Glancing at Jeff as he drove me to the airport so that I could catch my flight to Florida, I thought, "How concerned he must be, to say the least, about what has transpired since April." His life was being affected and I admired the strength he showed as he allowed me to make this journey without showing how upsetting this must be to him. He was very supportive and showed concern in a very caring, controlled way, so as not to discourage me. God was really watching over us, and his guidance was like he was really walking hand in hand with us, keeping things fairly stable on the home front in spite of what was happening.

The gratitude I feel towards Jeff and for his being with me, through all the uncertainties, is a living testimony that two people can witness each other's life without having to control the other, and that love and marriage can survive a magnitude of changes!

April had planned to fly in from Texas and I would be coming from Minneapolis. We were going to meet at a designated hotel in Tampa, Florida and drive down along the coast together. By now, April and I had become quite good friends, but our relationship had developed over the phone. The plan was to stay in Tampa one night and then drive on down to Peace River and check into the hotel. We would be meeting Sandy upon arrival, and then take her class, Psychic Development 1.

During the flight to Tampa, I had a "feeling" that I needed to call my sister, Bonnie. By now, I have learned that whenever I got a "feeling," it was a good idea to pay attention! There I was, on a plane half way between Minneapolis and Tampa, and the song "Moon River" started playing in my head. The words "just around the bend" stood out as the song repeated. As the music played, the feeling to call became stronger and stronger. I now started hearing, "Perhaps you should call." "Okay," I thought. "I can't use a cell phone, I can't send up smoke signals and the only option was the expensive phone on the back of the airplane seat." I had learned by then, though, that when a message comes through so strongly, I didn't have to be Einstein to figure out that I ought to pay attention, even though I could choose not to.

I chose to pick up the phone and call my sister Bonnie. Up to that point, she was the sibling who had been somewhat supportive about this trip and she was the only one I was having any conversations with. The phone rang and she answered. The first question she asked was, "How did you know to call me?" She continued, "I just got off the phone with Mother, and I am really wondering if what you are doing is something you should do."

We talked for a moment and she mentioned that she started doubting her support of me whenever she talked to Mom or someone in the family because they were so concerned. I then heard a voice tell me that she should get the "watch." I asked Bonnie what that meant. She said her watch stopped when Wayne died. She went and got it. As I asked her to look at the time, she exclaimed, "It moved! It hasn't moved since that day!" Just as she said that, the hands moved again. I thought, "Wow, that is pretty cool!" I told her about the music I heard and the words "just around the bend." She laughed and said that the song always reminded her of Wayne. And I replied, "Well, I think there is a message in this." She agreed, and wished me well on my journey to Florida.

I didn't understand it at the time, but it seems that Wayne and Friar were working very hard to help set up a support system for me as I journeyed ahead. I was slowly learning to take those leaps of faith and learn to trust in what I was receiving.

I had heard several times from friends and family, "How lucky! I wish that I had Wayne with me." I kept thinking how bittersweet it was. I love him so much; he is my big brother and I can see and hear him, but I can no longer get those hugs or feel him like I did when he was on the physical world. After he passed, I really missed that, and in fact grieving was difficult for me, because he was around me so much. I still miss his physical presence.

At an event that Christie and I were doing in November, 2003, I sat down before going on stage and had a discussion with Wayne. I said something like this, *"Wayne, I offer you gratitude for all that you have been, are, and will be to me on every level. If I am in any way holding you here or holding you back from something you need to do, please know that I release this tie we have. But if you are choosing to be a source of guidance for me, you are always welcome."*

Since then, I have worked with Friar and other guides, but Wayne's timing has, is, and, I believe, always will be impeccable. I continue to welcome his visits and am truly grateful for his past, present, and future guidance as well as for the trust he has helped me develop and the connections that he has helped me make. He has never steered me wrong, either from this side or from the other.

His wife, Marian, gave me one of his rosaries and I carry it with me when I work. That rosary signifies the beginning and the development of this journey, and is a gentle reminder from a brother that guidance is all around us, even in moments when we choose not listen.

PART II
the Calling

PEACE RIVER
and ME

*"Living life by acknowledging synchronicities
is like having a divine blue print!"*

The anticipation of the third weekend in June, 2002, the weekend of Sandy Anastasi's class, had been overwhelming. My stomach was full of butterflies as the wheels of the airplane touched down at Tampa International Airport. I smiled, remembering that I had packed my suitcase over a week and a half before I had to leave Minnesota and that I'd had trouble sitting through a meal, or remembering what I needed to get at the grocery store without my mind wandering. What would it be like meeting Sandy and being with people who were seeking knowledge similar to what I sought?. As the airplane doors opened, I realized, "I am actually here!"

After my trip to New Orleans and all the lessons I had learned every day since then, my intentions had changed dramatically and I didn't keep this a secret. I no longer had any desire to shut off the visits. This desire was replaced with a hope and excitement that I would continue to develop trust in the guidance I was receiving and be able to cross any hurdles that I might meet. I now had a larger mission. I found what made my heart sing and now my heart was playing my song. I found that child within and she and I were about to embark on a lifetime of growth and evolution. As Joseph Campbell is quoted on a picture I have, "We must be willing to let go of the life we planned, to have the life that is awaiting us."

It was time to get off the plane and head to the hotel. In June, the Florida weather was quite a bit warmer than Minnesota's, but the ocean and ocean breeze were wonderful and cooling amenities! April decided to meet me in the airport's baggage claim area. For a moment, I found myself thinking that I had never in my life shared a room with someone I didn't know well. As I came down the escalator, I saw her. She was waiting for me, with her smile cheek-to-cheek, her dark hair pushed behind her ears, and her eyes dancing. It almost felt as if two young kids were getting together for a summer adventure, we were both so excited! We hugged, picked up our luggage, and headed to the hotel in Tampa.

April and her husband, Eric, had gone to college together, more or less growing up together. April is of Native American heritage and she is openly very proud of it. When I met her, she had three grown children and what she referred to as an "acquired" daughter. At that time her two sons were in college out West, and I found it interesting that her daughter was in Minneapolis going to college at the University of Minnesota. The daughter April "acquired" when the girl was nineteen was in California. Eric had passed away from complications due to ulcerated colitis.

We stayed at a Holiday Inn close to the Tampa Bay area, near the water. We decided to have dinner out on the terrace that faced the water. The weather was pleasant and the light calming when, close to sunset, we selected a table. April mentioned that she could see Eric but could not hear him. As we ate dinner, I noticed that Eric was sending information. I shared with her that Eric kept giving me the feeling, "I can't take my eyes of the waitress's waistline." She commented that it was his favorite part on a woman to look at. "Great," I thought, smiling, "Does that tendency in men ever change?" It really is a great example of how spirits communicate information about their physical life and their attitudes while alive. And this tends to help the person on this side recognize the spirit from the other side.

I have found that people on the other side usually display information in a way that the person with whom they are communicating will understand. Eric's comment about the waitress's waistline was his way of getting April's attention.

That evening, April and I shared stories about our families and experiences. We both carried sadness over recent losses. For April, her sadness was attached to her husband, and for me, it was about Wayne. We also shared the experience of receiving a certain amount of static from particular family members about what we were doing.

Prior to Eric's passing, April hadn't seen people on the other side, nor did she have an interest in the subject matter. The night after Eric died, though, he appeared in her bedroom. She was unable to hear him but could see him. He appeared as if he was speaking. Her mother, had moved in with April and Eric the fall prior to Eric's passing and who had helped April through Eric's final problems and was now supporting April emotionally. She had also seen Eric in the house. The third time Eric appeared was at his visitation. He was seated in the first pew in the balcony of the church and, by the look she saw on his face, April felt that he was quite pleased that his family had come together from great distances.

April was now interested in communicating with the other side, but her family was concerned for her. They were suspicious because she was so interested in a topic she hadn't been interested in before.

April was working through the loss and the loneliness that comes with losing a partner. She seemed to want validations regarding her future. She asked me if I felt she would ever marry again or have a boyfriend. "So here it goes," I thought. "I must be doing a reading." I told her that Eric was around to help both of them heal the issues they had between them. Eric wasn't always the kindest person to her when he was alive, it seems, but he loved her deeply.

As I listened to him and others, I picked up a lot of information quickly. I told her that I felt she would be traveling to the Northeast soon. She said that she was going to a class reunion in that area. I then shared with April that there was a man there who she would reconnect with and who she'd have a long-term relationship with. I also told her that I saw her making a physical move from Texas to New York. I even saw her relationship with the man develop into marriage or a lifelong relationship. She said there had been a young man who she was crazy about earlier in her life, and she was hoping to reconnect with him. I commented that I felt this situation was probably what I was seeing. And I let her know that Eric was giving her the thumbs-up.

I asked April if she could see the Monk, she replied, "Yes!" I then asked her if she could help me find out his name, as I wasn't getting that from him. When I pushed the issue, I only saw the Monk holding his hand up and backing away. She laughed and said, "Yeah, his name is Stephen." Well, that made sense, since my oldest son is named Steven. I found it difficult to call him a name similar to that of my first-born son, who at the time was neither thrilled nor pleased to hear that his mother was taking on this adventure. It was at this point I started calling the Monk "Friar."

April offered another validation for me through her abilities; she could see and hear my brother and his laughter, Friar, as well as others on the other side. I often think back to this weekend and remark how guides from the other side really seek ways to catch your attention and draw you closer to them. I wondered why April could hear Friar's name when he didn't share it with me, and why she could hear Friar but not Eric. I now realize that April didn't want to hear Eric until she could let go of her pain and anger about his leaving her. For me, Friar's first goal was to capture my attention and have me listen to him. Perhaps there also was some emotional block that stopped me from hearing his name.

The next morning we headed south along the west coast of Florida to Port Charlotte, with our destination being the Holiday Inn across Peace River. As we set out, I was excited: It was as if I were "going home." I could not really place the feeling, but it stayed with me during our two-hour trip.

We decided to stop in Port Charlotte, where Sandy's store is, before heading to the hotel. As we entered the store, Starchild, I noticed it felt "tight," with an almost muffled feeling. I now think that those feelings were in response to the amount of protection that Sandy and her employees put around the store.

We walked around the store looking at the books and merchandise set up in the main part of the store. The other side was the classroom and a coffee shop. We didn't see Sandy right away because she was in her office doing a reading.

I was taken back by the display of Wiccan items and things used for divination in one corner. My response was triggered by one of my old fears. Growing up, I had been scared by stories of witches and goblins I had seen on television, and I guess that fear stuck with me.

As I looked further around the store, I saw a man behind the counter. He seemed reserved, as if he found safety behind the glass cases and wasn't crazy about being in close contact with his customers. He was tall with a medium build, brown eyes, brown hair, and was slightly bald. I remember wondering what wounds he carried that would encourage him to "hide." I remember I didn't particularly care for him, and I sensed that it was somewhat mutual. I had the feeling that he was cynical and unhappy. I wasn't sure why I had those feelings.

A woman stepped out of the office and, as I turned, I recognized Sandy immediately. She greeted me, and I noticed that she looked just like the image I had of her when we spoke on the phone. Sandy is about 5'8" tall, with long blond hair, and eyes that looked at me intensely. She struck me as observant, friendly, and welcoming. There was something very familiar about Sandy, but at the time I really had no idea what it was. She introduced the man behind the counter as her partner, John Maerz. I was a little uncomfortable as I felt her psychically reading information about me as we were conversing. I felt intruded upon, but I heard Wayne and Friar say, "Allow her." Apparently, she was sizing up her new students. She asked how our trip was and where we were staying. I was elated to be there with her, in person.

April and I left the store and drove over the Peace River bridge on our way to the Holiday Inn, where we were to spend three days. As we went over the bridge, the name of the street signs stood out as if they were illuminated by neon lights. At the first intersection was "Olympia". I later learned I had a Greek protector guide on the other side. The next street, and the one we were to turn on, was named "Marian," which is the name of Wayne's wife. At the next turn, there was an old gas station that had changed into a florist shop. The structure was a small building, and its two-pillared gas pump area closely resembled the Pure Oil station by the park in Plainview that I had walked by a thousand times growing up.

We finally arrived at the Holiday Inn. I realized, given the street names and the station; why I'd had the feeling that I was "coming home." What an enormous validation that the other side was really at work supporting me! Synchronicities were happening at quite a pace!

We went to dinner at the restaurant in the hotel and retired early to our room. Class was starting at 10 a.m., so it was time to unpack and get ready for the morning. I went to the vending machine and looked out the window. What I saw has become a symbolic scene that I now rely on every day. It was just around the time the sun was setting. Looking out over the water, I saw two bridges spanning about a mile across Peace River, connecting Port Charlotte to the north and Punta Gorda to the south. The hotel is on the Punta Gorda side, looking out at the water in between the bridges and towards Port Charlotte. The hotel has a small dock that is situated between the two bridges. To the left, as I looked out, I saw the sun setting; above the West bridge were clouds that formed the shape of an eagle, reminding me of my brother. He was in the Air Force and was very proud of his service. I ran back to the room to get April and share with her what I was seeing.

Later that weekend, on the Sunday morning before class, I walked down to the dock to enjoy the view. As I was standing there, I was again taken back by the view. The water was as smooth as glass. As I looked up to the bridge that had traffic going North, and thought, "Wow, this reminds me of friends and family and other people driving in the fast lane as they go through life. They are not looking at the beauty all around them that is so close at hand, including the beautiful sunrises like the one just above this bridge. Looking at the world this way, I thought, truly shows how fragile and fleeting life can be.

I envisioned the other bridge as carrying us as we journey after death, as holding all of the loved ones—relatives and friends—who have passed on. Using this symbol of the bridge, I thought, helps us envision them still here. The need to slow down and feel their presence in the here and now is ever present.

When I first saw the bridges from the hotel window, the sky above held a beautiful sunset, full of oranges, yellows and reds. I later learned that, during the day, seagulls and pelicans dive in the water between the bridges and fly above. When you sit on the dock, quietly reflecting in the moment or meditating, you can see dolphins jump and the manatee and other river creatures swim. The dolphins follow the boats up river from the ocean.

That Sunday morning as I watched the cars speed over the bridge, I noticed that people were so busy racing around that they were missing the center, the beauty that surrounded them. For me, this image represents people with their minds filled with thoughts about the past or the future, who are forgetting that there is also the present. That morning, seeing the calm water and the beauty of the peaceful river as well as the chaos of the highway, I truly felt that I was in the moment.

Today, I use this image in visualization to bring balance to my day and to slow down. It is there, in the midst of those two bridges, that I can help others and myself. In this calm area, I look forward to being as much as I can be!

I will forever be grateful to Wayne for directing me to Peace River and these two bridges.

SCHOOL *is* *in* SESSION

*"It is when we allow our eyes to open
that we see the beauty in all of God's creation."*

On the Saturday of my weekend in Florida, Friar and Wayne gave me my 4 a.m. wake-up call. I thought groggily, "I live in the Central Time zone and now I am in the eastern time zone and they still call precisely at 4 a.m. No extra hour with those guys!" By that time, though, I had learned that I enjoy waking up and hearing what they have to say. Even though once and awhile I am tired, I have found that it is better for me just to get up, because when I try to force myself back to sleep, I generally awaken with a sick headache feeling. Besides, they usually have a lot to talk about, and I look forward to our conversations. I feel that they are always communicating, and it is my choice to listen. And yes, I know that early morning is an important part of the day! So, why would I want to miss it?

Getting up, I sat by the patio window looking out at the sight of Peace River and felt enormous anticipation. In only a couple of hours I would be sitting in a psychic development class, watching Sandy do her work.

I looked across the room. The woman that I had met just a few weeks prior lay asleep in her bed. I have never shared a room with a stranger or someone I had known so briefly in the past. I thought of the changes that were occurring and was amazed that I was actually there.

Then as I gazed back at Peace River, a sense of sadness rushed through me as I thought of Christine back home. We had shared so much, and I felt uncomfortable that she was not with me. After all, she was the adventurous one, not me. At least she was taking the class on tape, and we would work together when I returned home. It seemed like no matter what I told myself, I still missed her being with me, and sharing Peace River and all that I was discovering here.

As I looked out over the river, my thoughts turned to how my reasons for being in Florida had changed since my phone call to Sandy. I wondered what it would be like in class. What would the other people who were attending be like? What would happen in class and what do Sandy and her business partner/husband, John Maerz, do during class?

My thoughts drifted next to my brother, Wayne, and to Friar. How hard they must be working, keeping me busy taking all the leaps of faith that brought me here! They kept me so safe that they must have been the wind beneath my wings.

Dealing with this weekend—probably the first of many such weekends—would be the next big leap of faith. Signing on with Sandy meant embracing the commitment to return here every month for as long as I felt I needed to. The classes were estimated to last 6 months if you attended the whole series. It would mean a trip every month, and paying the $125.00–$150.00 tuition plus the costs of airfare, hotel, rental car, and expenses. I had been so busy the last few months, and now the expenses would be stacking up. For someone who was not working, taking on this commitment would be a huge leap of faith. This venture was so compelling to me, and I had so much passion in my heart for it, that I did not see any alternatives except to be there and do it!

With only little money but a heart full of faith, I embarked on this part of my journey knowing that at any moment the funds might run out and I would have to stop. It was a big leap of faith to put aside the fear of this reality, and have faith that everything would work out if it all was meant to be. It meant being willing to open myself up enough to see the possibilities rather than staying in a place of worry and want, a place I had stayed in for most of my life.

I felt a new viewpoint emerging. I began working from a place of letting go and allowing everything to unfold, looking forward through faith, and recognizing each miracle, big or small. I think it was Einstein who said something like "Either you believe there are no miracles or everything is a miracle." And for me, everything was absolutely a miracle!

April eventually woke up, and we got ready for the big day. We had breakfast in the hotel restaurant. As we sat there, I was able to spend a little more time taking in the wonderful view of Peace River. What a great place to have breakfast. Our heads were filled with thoughts of what the day might hold for us.

As we drove across the east bridge, traveling north to Starchild, I felt like a child going to her first day of school. I was fifty-two years old, and experiencing this wonderful feeling. My heart leapt in anticipation.

Sandy had asked her students to drive around to the back of the store to park their cars for the day. As we got out of the car, I noticed that there were many others there. I wondered how many students there would be and what they would be like. As we entered through the back of what was then the "Constellation Coffee Shop," we went to the side of the store that held the weekend and evening classes. Sandy was busy greeting people and selling beverages from behind a counter. As I glanced around the room, I saw one shelf lined with books and bellydancing items. As my eyes glanced out the windows along the front, I noticed there were a few chairs outside and over to the side there was a dry erase board. To my right was a piano, more shelves lined with books, and the two french doors that were closed when classes were in session. On the other side of the doors were shelves lined with different types of incense and other, similar items.

In the store part of the shop, John Maerz was busy behind his counter. The display shelves made a square as if to keep him safe from the demanding customers who were waiting to pay for their class. He was wearing glasses low on his nose and looked like the proverbial "shopkeeper." He concentrated intently on adding up the payments from the students. It appeared to be a busy day at Starchild.

I noticed that the average age of the students was probably forty-something. There were about twenty students, and only a few were men. There were several women who seemed as if they were single or alone, a few who looked as if they had their finances figured out, and some who looked as if they were barely able to make it there because of finances or daycare issues. Most of the women appeared rather educated and appeared to know more about "psychic stuff" than I did. Some had traveled more than 150 miles, some much further, and there were a few local residents.

Remembering that I had not had much experience with psychics or their abilities to read people, I had this nagging feeling that Sandy was "in our heads," reading her students and finding out what they were dealing with. At the time, I didn't understand why I felt that way, but it was something that really drew my attention. What I was certain about was that she was confident, friendly, and very good at working with a variety of people.

We learned that each monthly class consisted in a two-day course that usually ran from morning until 5 p.m. This course was the first, or beginner's level, course on psychic development.

When Sandy and John sat down in the front of the room, all eyes focused on them. Class was now officially in session.

They started the class with a short introduction about their backgrounds, telling us about the years of experience they had in the field. Sandy shared with the class that she was born in Long Island, New York, has the sun sign Gemini, and had a BS degree from Adelphi University. She had a colorful work history, ranging from being a teacher to a safety engineer, and stated that she had almost twenty years experience in the metaphysical field.

After the introduction, the class did its first meditation. John Maerz led the students through a ten-point relaxation, similar to the one the Monroe Institute and many therapists use for self-hypnosis and relaxation, and then a group meditation. When the students were done with the first meditation, everyone looked as if he or she had just received a great massage. John led all the meditations that were presented throughout the series, and this weekend we did approximately six meditations.

While John Maerz led the meditations, Sandy did most of the instructing, though John interjected where and when he felt it was appropriate. They appeared to be fairly in sync with each other as the class moved through the meditations. The meditations became easier as we progressed through the weekend. It felt good getting to the point where there was no outside interference, including no voices, no intrusions. That is, until I felt Sandy tapping into me again. I had no idea what this meant, but it felt like someone was peeking into me. I was very curious why Sandy tapped into each of us as we were doing the lessons.

I later asked Sandy why I felt that way, and she validated that, for beginning students, the whole experience is like learning to ride a bike with her as the training wheels. Each student ends up on their own, but she helps them get their feelings going, so that they can practice and develop their psychic abilities themselves.

She mentioned that I was the only one that had caught on, and that this fact intrigued her. I was excited to have my feelings and experiences validated and to know what it felt like to have someone else "tap into" me!

As Sandy taught her information on sending and receiving messages, I found it interesting that she referred to the right side as the sending or male side, and the left side as the receiving or female side. It made sense and validated my experience, since my parents would touch my left arm when they wanted to get their point across. I also found their explanation of how to send an image or picture to your partner, and how it was important to let go of the image in your mind interesting, as well.

The information about sending and receiving information was followed by a psychic development aptitude test. We were informed that we were going to be sending and receiving shapes and colors. I have never taken tests with ease. Tests have always been a challenge for me. When April and I worked on the exercise, we found it easier if we treated it like a game. We were given a deck of cards. Each card had either the shape of a star, circle, rectangle or square on it. The cards had both plain and colored shapes. When the test was over, and I must add I felt great relief when it was over, I was surprised at how many correct answers I had given.

In one of the meditations, we were instructed to build a work place. The work place would be a place on the inner plane or in our mind where we would feel safe to practice some of the techniques they were going to be teaching us. With our mind's eye, we imagined ourselves in this place when we worked on childhood fear elimination and past life regression. Many of us have heard about therapists using these activities to help their patients. It was interesting to do the exercises. For me, it was as if I were actually viewing a video of events from my childhood, and given the chance to resolve issues associated with them. I now understand first hand the benefit that psychologists and therapists bring to their patients when they implement these techniques with clients.

April saw her work place as a teepee, and for me it was a place with huge windows that looked out onto a liberating white expanse. That weekend we also did some miscellaneous exercises, including remote viewing and dream interpretation.

Upon completion of the last meditation of the weekend, I opened my eyes and looked at John Maerz. For some reason, the face of one of my grandsons, my oldest son's boy, was superimposed over John's face and my forehead hurt. I had no idea what it meant. I didn't say anything, because Sandy and John were busy saying goodbye to the students and I thought I could talk to Sandy later about it. I felt uneasy seeing Nathan's face transposed over John's and not knowing what it meant. I was concerned about Nathan, but didn't know how I could mention this to my son without it causing him alarm.

As April and I were about to leave class, Sandy walked over to me, raised her hand, and gently brushed her fingers against the hair on my forehead as she said with kindness, "Susan, if I was going to do a reading for you, I would make your oldest son, the one with hair like yours, pay for it. Don't worry about what he thinks—he has his own issues going on."

In a polite way, she was letting me know that she was aware of the strife I was having with my family over coming to Florida and attending the class. It was also a validation that what I felt was correct. But at the same time, it was a little unnerving, given that I hadn't shared with her any information about my children! I walked away thinking, "She is one of the most fascinating people I have ever met."

When I work with clients or students, I think about the encouragement I felt from my mentor, and I pray that I will be that for each of my students. It was a true act of guidance. True mentors do not do the work for you, but are there to guide you!

I was struck again that there was something about Sandy that felt very familiar, but at the time I didn't know why. I remember feeling sad as I walked out of the classroom and I could not place why, but I knew that it was there and I felt like I was saying goodbye to someone who, though new to me, felt like an old friend. I also felt as if I were leaving home, even though I knew I wanted to go back home to my husband and family. I remember all those intense feelings well.

April and I headed up to New Port Ritchie, where I was going to drop her off at her friend's home where she planned to stay for a few days. After dropping her off, I was going to head for Tampa to catch my flight.

April and I promised each other that we, and Christine, would work on the homework exercises every day. We were going to send and receive objects and scenes several times a week.

After I dropped her off, I was driving by a McDonalds Restaurant when I felt the urge to stop. No, it wasn't for food, but I pulled into the lot and felt an uncanny urge to open the trunk of the car. All of a sudden, I felt like something warm was dripping from my forehead; my forehead hurt and my clothes felt dirty or soiled. I saw myself sitting in the classroom looking at John Maerz as he had my grandson's face superimposed over his! I had this uncontrollable feeling I had to get clean clothes out and change into them. After all the things that had been happening, I did just that!

When my plane landed in Minneapolis, I called my son to find out that my grandson, Nathan, had fallen and hit his head. He had required stitches and was probably getting them when I felt that strong compulsion to change my clothes. What a coincidence! Or was it? I e-mailed Sandy the next day to ask her what she thought about what had happened. She said that she felt that I was connected with my grandson and that perhaps I had felt what was happening to him and maybe even helped lessen the injury.

This event about Nathan was similar to others that had happened to me. As a child, I thought perhaps I caused things to happen instead of realizing that I was experiencing a psychic connection to an event that was taking place or was going to happen. When I was a child, I didn't understand how or what was happening, but I sure felt guilty about it. Even though I couldn't figure out logically how I could have caused events to happen when I wasn't even there, I still sang the song, "what if I caused it."

But there was one major difference now: I was able to identify my experience and see it in a different way. With Friar and Wayne speaking loud and clear, I knew I could learn from the experience and let it go. I would like to believe I had the experience in order to lessen the injury for Nathan, but even if I didn't, having the experience gave me a new level of understanding about "psychic sight" and taught me that my guilt was really about seeing something that was going to take place and not having the ability to prevent it from happening. This in itself was a major realization for me. In my opinion, it was a pivotal experience that showed me the way to heal some very old wounds and prevent future ones.

It had only been eight weeks since Wayne passed away and my intentions had changed dramatically, especially given my experiences in New Orleans and in the class with Sandy. I had no doubt that I would be on this path of discovery for as long as I was physically able to!

For the first time in my adult life I wasn't focused on my children's needs and accepted that they were all grown, married, and doing well. This was going to be a time for me to heal the issues that I carried through life, and it would be a time of self-discovery. I didn't dwell on what might prevent me from continuing this quest, but took the leaps of faith so that I could progress on my path. Wayne and Friar may not have explained everything, but I knew that I trusted them and I knew that I was in God's hands. In fact, as time went on, money seemed to be there when I needed it. Sometimes it showed up literally at the last minute.

The timing of these developments in my life was exquisite. It was a time when my kids were involved with their own children and in their own lives, and Jeff and I were in a place of trust and support.

April had already agreed to continue with me through the classes and we were planning our trip for the weekend in July, when we would be in Class 2. Learning that Christie would be able to go with us made our plans perfect.

Christine and I continued doing the practical lessons Sandy and John had taught in class and on tape. I was working with Christie and we were so grateful to find something that made us both so happy! And we now had April to work with as well. My days were filled with doing the sending and receiving exercises with Chris, and I did them several times a week with April. They were vital to our psychic development for several reasons. First, you get immediate validation when someone gets what you sent or you receive an image from them. Practicing these exercises also taught us to distinguish between the feeling of telepathy, the feeling of empathy readings, and channeling. I liked channeling when we were taught it, and practicing it helped me know how to put a label on what I did best. Our practice gave us a comparison to work from.

April's strongest ability at the time was telepathy. She had a very strong mind and students witnessed her ability to send what she chose to send them. She has strengthened her telepathic skills even more since then, and she has developed her reading and channeling abilities as well.

Christine's strongest ability was in channeling. I appreciated how really neat it was that we both are strong mediums. Channeling is the art of connecting with the eternal you or your higher self. You receive the best information from your higher self. It is harder to get immediate validation for information that you channel, however, because sometimes you can't know if the information is correct until some event in the future happens. However, as Christie's and my channeling abilities have developed, our clients often call and share with us their stories of validations about our readings. I am happy that our talents have helped them see more possibilities in their live and that they used the information that we gave them.

Meditations were daily rituals, and we were using protection meditations and exercises that Sandy and John Maerz discussed during our class and that John Edward taught on his tapes. My favorite was, and still is, the shower technique that John Edward teaches. You envision the white light of God pouring down over you washing all the negativity down the drain. You rinse yourself off, visualizing the white light filling you with positive energy and surrounding you protectively.

Sandy and John taught us to use sea salt in a bath as a way to cleanse and protect, and I enjoyed these baths more when I learned I could add essential oils to the sea salt. Surrounding myself in a protective bubble when I needed to feel safe was an added way to ensure my safety.

Often, Christine and I felt the urge to go out on "outings," the reasons for which we never really knew when we first felt the urges. Though the reasons for our missions were never clear to us initially, we always accepted them and the reasons for the missions became clear when we were done. We also experienced urges to call people, and when we followed through, it always turned out to be "coincidences." The more we practiced the art of "being aware," the more it became obvious that we were receiving information. When we listened to it and acted on it, we always saw positive results.

It was becoming apparent that our guides were working full time with Christine and me, and with April. Now with the support from people at Starchild, it seemed that we had a network supporting us. Christie and April seemed very confident in what they were doing. As for me, I wavered, asking "Is it possible?" and yet, I generally was more than happy to take a leap, and having faith turned out just as or better than I could have imagined! It now seemed to me that Friar, Wayne, and others were running me through the paces. They helped me remember and get used to the feelings of working with "psychic senses." Having this spiritual guidance was opening up all sorts of possibilities that would help me discover who I was and who I could become.

It was as if I was discovering different aspects of myself every day! I began to realize that I had put myself into a really tight box, and I recognized how rigid I had grown. Like so many people, I found myself in a place in my life where I was wondering, "What happened?"

I found myself in this new place and didn't know what would happen next! Fortunate for me, my faith in Wayne and his love for me was so strong that I was kept "safe" until I learned more about psychic development and why I was able to do what I could do. It was as if someone had awakened me and turned on the light!

Once when I was a little girl, I asked my mother to turn on the bathroom light for me. She was busy and replied, "You're okay, just go in there. The light is broken." Being a resourceful child, I ran to my brother, Wayne, and asked him if he would turn it on. He went into the bathroom and turned the light on. I ran back to my mother and in my little girl way of speaking, one that sometimes ran words together, I exclaimed, "Mommy, Mommy, nope-a-light-a-broke-a-nope!"

During this period when I was growing confident in my psychic abilities, Wayne reminded me of this story every chance he got. And it has been the one story that my large family reminds me of when we gather together. It is a story that has been repeated year after year, and I have carried it with me as a result. Well, was this another coincidence? Wayne, and the events around his passing, had turned that light on once again; nope-a-light-a-broke-a-nope!

Now that a month had passed since my first class at Starchild, it was time for Christine and me to prepare for the return trip to Florida. We'd both get to participate in the July 2002 Psychic Development 2. It felt so right that Christie was able to come along and meet Sandy and see Peace River. We arrived on Friday for the Saturday and Sunday class.

April was going to join us and it felt like we were the three psychic musketeers. Christine looked forward to seeing April. She hadn't seen her since New Orleans.

A SHAMAN
on the SCENE

*"Our inner light shines when we learn to
accept our differences rather than demand others
be who we want them to be."*

April met us at the airport earlier that Friday and all of us
were now settling into our room at the Holiday Inn at Peace
River. This time, our room was on first floor with a view right
between the two bridges. It became the room I stayed in on
almost every trip there. Christie enjoyed both the room and
the view.

April, Christie, and I decided to head over to Starchild to
share discoveries from our last trip with Christine. Though
we didn't know it at the time, as usual, it was going to prove
to be something more than I had bargained for.

Driving across the East Bridge toward Starchild, I felt the
exhilaration of being over Peace River with my daughter and
April, heading toward our next adventure. It felt more

complete with Christie present and the energy of excitement was all about. I felt like we were glowing!

As we pulled into the parking lot outside of Starchild, Christie took note of the front of the store, with the name "Starchild" in neon lights. You could see the sparkle in her eyes.

As we enter the store, there were a few people mingling and looking around. John Maerz struck his usual pose behind the counter, looking up over the top of the glasses that were positioned low on his nose. I walked up and introduced Christie to him. He gave a small smile and said hello. He quickly returned to his work. I felt he was being polite at best, but neither of us had much interest in the other. As Sandy came around the corner, she seemed her usually friendly self and greeted us. She talked to Christie for a while and we just perused the store, taking in all there was to see.

Christie later commented that she felt a little uncomfortable in the store. She said that she felt the presence of Ancient Egypt and pyramids, and that it made her uncomfortable. She then said that she felt uncomfortable with both Sandy and John, but she couldn't really say why, since there was no obvious reason for her discomfort.

It was getting to be late afternoon and, still in the shop, we were talking about what to eat for dinner. We were looking at the class schedules and noticed a class called "Shamanic Healing," which started later that evening at 7 p.m. The girls speculated about what the class might entail and, as I listened to what they were saying, I realized I had no clue what they were talking about. I knew about physicians, chiropractors, and a little about oriental medicine practitioners, but what was shamanic healing?

As Christie and April continued talking, the shop's glass door opened and a man walked in. He had long brown-grayed hair, was wearing black hot pants, a tight shirt that showed off his muscular build, a band of leather around his arm accentuating his arm muscles, and a white derby. He was carrying a black date book. He definitely drew attention to himself and I could certainly feel the power of his presence. In fact, I could feel the energy and excitement in the room build as the women checked him out. I heard April and Christie talking about signing up for his class on shamanic healing.

When they asked me if I'd join them, I said, "Why would I want to do that?" Christie, with her "Oh, come on Mom" coaxing, and April, with that big grin she makes when she is being cute, were trying their best to persuade me. I remember thinking I was being out-voted and then I heard Wayne say, "Oh come on, it will be a great experience." So, a little reluctantly, I agreed to take this class from the man whose name turned out to be Mic McManus.

We ran out for a quick bite to eat and returned to the rear classroom at Starchild for the class. I think I picked the chair closest to the door so that, if I felt like I needed to make an early exit, I could. It looked like there were about ten students: eight women and two men.

As I glanced around the room, I noticed a massage table in the front. Now I was curious. What were they going to use that for, and what would we be expected to do? The only place I had seen one of those was in a spa when I had a massage. Hmm… I really had no idea what we were going to do.

Mic McManus entered the room and shut the door. As he proceeded to the front of the room, I noticed he had put on long black pants, but that this was the only thing that changed. As he began to introduce himself, I noticed his New York accent as he talked about working as a healer. He had been to the jungles of Peru to study with a shaman named

Don Augustine Rivas. He made it clear that he was planning to return to Peru in the near future.

The room felt full of energy and warmth. He had everyone's undivided attention, especially that of the women. As he shared anecdotes about his experiences as a healer and told us that he was also a Reiki Master, I couldn't help but notice that he had everyone in the palm of his hand.

He taught the basics of healing and how to allow the healing energy to flow from your hands. His teaching technique was different from Sandy's. He asked a student what she wanted healed and everyone gathered around, placing their hands over the person on her feet, knees, hands, elbows, shoulders and head. And then, everyone sent energy to the person, directing the healing to the area she wanted. In Sandy's classes, we were learning healing through remote viewing, which means that you envision the person with whom you are working, and you send streams of energy to them. You then envision cutting off the energy stream and clearing the space between you and the person receiving the energy.

A person with a back problem got off the table after a healing and exclaimed how much better her back felt. When it was my turn to lie on the table, I asked if they could work on my right ankle. I could feel the warmth of the energy as it entered my body at the point of each set of hands. My ankle felt warm and tingly, and when the flow of energy stopped, it didn't hurt. The same thing happened with someone who was having knee pain that night. The same pattern continued with each of the students as Mic moved back and forth, using sacred tobacco and moving his healing energy to the place the student directed it. He used tobacco that he brought back from Peru. It looked like the actual leaves that are laid out to dry. After he uses it in ceremonies, Mic then puts the pieces in his pipe.

This was a basic introductory class. But after about the first three minutes, I was totally interested in what I was feeling and seeing. I could see waves of energy move around and across the students; the light in the room seemed to be whiter and the air clearer. The space had a feeling of comfort, warmth, and security!

When the class ended, I asked Mic if he did private healing sessions and he said yes. He couldn't schedule one at Starchild during the weekend workshops or on Mondays when the shop closed. I told Mic that it would be difficult for me to schedule time with him, since I only came into town for the weekend. He asked me to follow him outside.

Once outside, he gave me his business card and phone number. We made plans to meet at his Sarasota home to do a healing session for each of us. My appointment would be on Sunday evening, when all three of us girls would go together.

We retired back to the hotel that night with thoughts of the class with Sandy and John that would start tomorrow and made plans to go to Sarasota to meet with Mic Sunday night.

At 4 a.m., I heard the chatter of distant voices. I opened my eyes slowly and saw the faraway lights that line the West Bridge spanning Peace River. I had left the glass balcony door open the previous night and could now hear the rhythm of the water as it rolled against the pillars of the pier. For a moment, I didn't want to move; I just wanted to enjoy the sounds and the feeling of my surroundings.

Christie and April were still asleep and it felt comfortable to know they were there and yet have this moment to take in the peacefulness I felt, here at Peace River.

As I got up to go to the patio, I noticed how the bridge lights reflected on the water. They seemed like an endless stream of light over the water. There was a stuffed chair that was in front of the patio door and I found it very comfortable as I closed my eyes to listen to sounds.

With my eyes closed and focused on the sounds, I found myself conversing with the other side. I was asking Wayne, Friar, and others who were guiding me to please help me today. I was grateful for the opportunity to be there and yet I felt an uneasiness about going to class later that day. I was praying for help, to bring understanding to me in what I was going to learn that weekend. I felt a lot of anticipation, though Christie and April appeared so confident; I wondered when it would be like that for me.

My thoughts went to my family back home. I thought of the family members who disapproved of my choice to seek knowledge about what I was going through, and I thought of my husband, who must have felt my absence in the bed next to him. I felt myself missing him and Josie, our Dalmatian, who filled our home with her unconditional love and spontaneity. I felt Wayne's hand on mine, and at that moment I knew I would be okay.

I decided to take my shower before the others awoke. Since we were three women with one bathroom, I thought we might need extra time to get ready for breakfast. As I approached the bathroom, I noticed the three knots in the door's wood. It made me smile, as there were three of us in the room, and then I heard Friar say, "It is also the number of the triad." I asked him what he meant and he replied, "Father, Son, and Holy Spirit."

The shower was a bit crowded that morning as Dad, my grandmas Tillie and Julia, Wayne, and Friar, let me know that they were proud of me. I found myself thanking them for being there and started envisioning God's white light surrounding me as the water poured over me. I felt all the negative feelings of doubt wash down the drain, and as I did, the bathroom seemed lighter and so did I.

After getting ready in the bathroom, I opened the door and Christie was now awake and wanting to get ready. It felt so good that she was there to share this weekend. We hugged as she went to get into the shower before April got up.

It was now light outside and I decided to take the bread I purchased the night before and feed the seagulls. As I stood on the sidewalk and opened the bread wrappers, I could hear the seagulls as they came closer. I stood out there throwing bread to them until all four loaves were gone. I was captivated by how some would swoop down to take the bread off the railing, while other's would get close enough to catch the bread in mid air and others just clamored out of fear and fought for each piece that fell to the water.

I found that each time one took a piece of bread out of mid air, my heart felt like it was lifted and lighter. It was a very good feeling and I really didn't understand it, but I knew the feeling was important enough to take note of at the time.

When I returned to the room, Christie was putting on her makeup and April was just finishing getting ready; they sounded chatty and happy. In moments, we would be ready to go for breakfast.

The conversation at breakfast was filled with excitement about Mic's class and our plans to go up to his home on Floyd Street in Sarasota the next night. We found ourselves talking about who wanted to do their healing first. It was unanimous: we would let him choose. All three of us were wondering what a private session would be like. We were all together, so we felt secure enough for this adventure into the unknown.

It was getting late and we had to get going to Starchild. We parked behind the store and entered through the back door. Once again, Sandy was behind the coffee shop counter delivering on her promise of a good cup of coffee, tea, or whatever we wanted. She was busy talking with the students milling around her. We entered the store part of Starchild, and there was John Maerz behind the counter. We took care of the business of paying our tuitions and went into the class-room to pick three chairs that were not right up front, but not too far in the back, either. We placed ourselves in the second row, on the left side of the room.

After putting down our purses and notebooks, we got up to look around. I noticed that Jason Oliver was teaching a mediumship class in the back classroom. I remember my attention drifting to the room often during that weekend. I would have loved to be in there, but his was the fifth class of the series, and we had to wait until we had taken a few more classes. Sandy had her rules in place after years of experience and wanted her students to have an understanding of the dynamics before taking the class.

The weekend's topic was "Energy and Auras." As Sandy took her place in the front of the room with John next to her, the class knew it was time to settle in.

Sandy and John designed their psychic development classes to build one upon the other and students needed to take the class in the proper order of succession. "Auras and Energy" was a perfect topic to follow last month's "Intro-duction to the Chakras." Reminding us that the chakras are the energy centers within our bodies, Sandy told us that the aura is the energy field that surrounds our body.

She touched lightly on the topic of mediumship and how spirits communicate through one's aura field. As she explained that mediumship is the art of spirit communication or connecting the physical and the spirit world through commu-nication, she drew a picture on the dry erase board of a silhouette of a body with a sort of bubble around it, representing the energy field she called the aura. She explained that we pick up signals from the other side that touch our aura, and pointed to the bubble she drew.

I raised my hand, because her explanation didn't match what I understood, and asked, "Sandy, if that is the way you feel they communicate, then why do I hear, see, and feel them?" Sandy very nicely said, "Susan, this is very basic information. You are here to learn why you can do what you do, not to learn how!" Everyone turned to look at me. As a person who does not like that kind of attention, I just wanted to sink back down in my chair very quietly.

I thought to myself, "What I felt early this morning was probably a sign of what was happening now." I guess somewhere inside of me I thought the students who talked about their psychic abilities were way out there ahead of me. I was stunned when she said those words. At the same time, I felt it set me up to have the other students take notice that I was in the room. It was a very uneasy moment for me. And my ego was a little worried. What if I didn't measure up to those expectations?

On break, I ran into Jason Oliver in the store area. I almost dragged him into the class room. I soon found out that Jason was willing to discuss the question I had raised in Sandy's class! I asked Jason the same question because I wanted his opinion about the difference between my experience of mediumship and her explanation of it.

Jason said, "Susan, when people start to develop their basic abilities, we first explain how it works so that students have a platform on which to work. That particular class doesn't address the more advanced way that you are communicating with the deceased. Don't worry about it; it will all make sense as you go through the rest of the classes."

I sat down in my chair and my mind was racing thinking about what Jason and Sandy said. In one sense, I felt assured that at some point I would probably bring it all together, but on the other hand, it gave students reason to talk about my background and abilities, and I felt there was a note of competition in the air. A few of the students were now standoffish.

During a later class in mediumship, I finally had enough nerve to ask Sandy about what she had said in this class. I remember her saying, "It was good to have the students stretch and your question set a standard in the room." I'm afraid her response did not make me feel any better.

Break was over and it was back to work. Sandy, the leader of the team of teachers in this course, asked that the students now pair off with someone they didn't know. A lady behind me grabbed my shoulder and asked if I minded if we paired off together. All the students now sat facing their partners. The lady and I sat knee to knee, facing each other.

We were going to do body scans. Sandy explained the technique; we were going to put our hands on top of our partner's hands, and take turns feeling our way through each other's bodies, psychically. We would start at our partner's head and work to the feet, noticing any differences in how we felt as we were doing it.

Our teachers were very insistent that we protected ourselves before we began. They stated that we should imagine putting on gloves or bracelets to stop anything from the other person from staying with us. I remember imagining stepping into a huge condom-like rubber suit, with a bubble at the top for my head, and zipping it up the back. It did look rather funny in my mind, but I wasn't going to take any chances! I was now ready to participate in the practical application.

My partner was a thin woman, probably in her late forties. She elected me to go first. I did the exact steps they taught us, and I felt my way through her body psychically. I didn't feel anything in the head area but when I reached her throat area I felt a huge lump in my throat; it built up until I felt I could hardly swallow. I shared with her that I felt she had trouble with her throat, perhaps with her thyroid, but also that she had trouble with her throat chakra. The next area that stood out was her abdominal area. I felt like I was missing my ovaries and uterus. Now that is pretty strange, because I don't usually feel them, but I now felt their absence. I went on to mention that I thought she had had a hysterectomy. And then I moved down her legs to her feet. I all of a sudden felt pain in my right foot and mentioned that I thought she was having trouble with her right foot. After completing this exercise, I remember thinking, "I hope I am close in the information!"

Well, it ended up that the reading I gave was 100 percent correct. Surprise! I passed. Boy, did I feel relief when I was done.

Before you do an exercise of this kind, it is important to know how your body feels before you start, and that it should feel the same way when you finish. You do not want to pick up someone else's issues! It was essential that we cleared ourselves of any feelings that were not ours. Some students shook their hands, like they were trying to shake off something that was stuck to them. Others ran their hands under water, and there were some who just felt they needed to lie with their spine on the ground for a moment or two.

Christie was paired with a gentleman. We had smiled at each other as we started. I thought, "Now you know the difference between men and women!" She picked up that he had back problems and knew the exact locations he had problems. I remember Christie talking about how her back actually hurt in the spots where his back hurt him. Christie also gave a reading that was 100 percent accurate.

April was paired with a lady who had red hair. She picked up the lady's elbow and shoulder problems. April also said that she felt pain in her body when she came to the areas that bothered her partner. April was 100 percent successful, too!

As we listened to the other students relate their experiences, I realized how much stuff we must be picking up about other people that we aren't even aware of. It is quite a benefit to our own well-being to know what is ours and what belongs to someone else!

We all had a lot of fun together this weekend, and we had quite a few "aha" moments! We all found that the meditations were much easier this weekend after practicing at home every day, prior to this class.

When the class ended on Sunday, we said our goodbyes. I remember walking over to Sandy to thank her for the weekend. As I looked into her eyes, she said, "I know Susan. I feel the same way." We hugged, and again I had the feeling of knowing her. It was funny that she agreed to what I was "thinking." I had been thinking that life is like a rollercoaster, and that I sure was happy to be there for this ride. I replied to Sandy, "I can't imagine not being here," and Sandy said, "Susan, I agree with you. Neither of us would miss the roller coaster ride!"

Later that afternoon, April, Christie, and I drove north to Sarasota to meet Mic at his home on Floyd Street. Christie and April were chatting about their weekend and the adventure we were now going on. I mentioned that I felt sad leaving the store for some reason. Christie said she felt it was because I just wasn't ready for the weekend to end. I think she was right. Luckily, I still had one more night on the river!

It took us about forty-five minutes by car to travel from Starchild to Floyd Street in Sarasota. It was a small street lined with trees and shrubs. Mic's navy blue car was parked in the driveway. As we approached the front of the house, we were all a bit nervous. None of us really had any expectations other than letting things happen. I reached forward and rang the doorbell. The door swung open and Mic greeted us with his welcoming smile and New York accent.

As we entered his house, the first thing I saw was a big copper object that appeared to be a series of copper pipes held together by balls of wood. It was in the shape of a dodecahedron and in the center of it is a massage table. In the room was a shelving unit holding crystals and candles. The candles were lit and I couldn't help but notice the aroma of nag champa incense in the air.

After removing our shoes at the front door, we walked through his living room, the room he used for doing his work, and into his dining room and kitchen area. Off to the side was what appeared to be a sitting room, complete with books and television.

The three of us sat with Mic around his kitchen table, where he showed us some of the crystals he had. Some were his favorites and others were for sale. Shanti, his cat, walked by, taking in the people who were sitting in his space. There was a picture of Mic and a woman with long red hair. He explained that Patti was his partner in life. She looked self-assured and had eyes that looked as if they were filled with heart-felt wisdom. I remember thinking what a stunning couple they made.

He offered us tea or water and a crystal book to look at while we waited our turns. April went first into the healing room. Christie and I looked at the crystals and worked on finding them in the book. I could hear the music of drums and jungle sounds as the healing was in progress. The smell of tobacco or something burning drifted into to kitchen as we sat waiting. Each healing took about forty-five minutes. When April reappeared, she looked relaxed and dazed.

Christie was next. As she was in the healing room, the drumming and jungle music played in the background. And once again, the smell of tobacco or something burning, was in the air.

April said that when Mic was working on her, she could feel something moving or washing through her. She said she felt her dad's presence and was working through something that had to do with her dad. We sat and looked through the book on crystals and looked at the Herkimer diamonds and other crystals that Mic had laid out for our viewing.

Forty-five minutes after Christie's healing started, she came back into the kitchen. Christie's face looked relaxed. She said she felt really good.

It was now my turn. As I entered the healing room, Mic lit a piece of white sage and fanned the smoke all about me with a feather. He said he was clearing my aura, or energy field. Upon completion of this task, he asked me to lie down on the table. In each of my hands he placed a stone. I asked him what they were; he replied that they were "bouji stones." He stated that their purpose was to help balance the female and male energy flow through my body. They felt cool; one seemed to be round and the other more oblong.

I laid down on the table, gazing through the top of the of the copper and wood dodecahedron. The light of the candles danced almost exactly to the rhythm of the drums and music in the background.

As he placed one hand on each of my shoulders, I saw my deceased brother, Wayne, standing to the right of me. I had not shared any story about my past with Mic, and I found it interesting that he brought up my brother's presence. As he began to move what felt like streams of air or energy about me, I started feeling calmer. I saw a tiny man standing on the other side of me and when I asked Mic who this was, he asked me to describe him. I explained that he had graying black hair and seemed to be from the jungle. He had a staff that he would hit on the floor. Mic just smiled and told me that it was the medicine man who helped him do his work. This man was not physically present in Mic's house, but nevertheless seemed busy at work helping him. It was a validating experience to learn that someone else again saw exactly what I saw. My first healing with Mic brought up my need to trust myself and what I saw. This sure was a great way to validate it!

I found Mic to be gentle and compassionate when he worked. This healing, and the work that followed with Mic over the next two years, were vital to my developing a true sense of what resonated for me. Trusting myself has always been a huge issue, and it was this healing that showed me a path that would lead to change. Before returning to the kitchen, Mic and I discussed the possibilities that I would spend a day or two more in Florida each month and begin to do more healing work with him. I knew it was an essential part of my journey.

When I returned to the kitchen, April and Christie were happily talking and were ready to go for dinner. It was our last night before departing for home. We paid Mic for his services and went on our way.

The conversation that evening included endless discussions about the weekend's discoveries. April shared with us that she was not going to be able to come down next month due to a family event that was taking place, but that she would be attending the forth class in the series.

As we packed our belongings in preparation for the next morning's return, I found my thoughts drifting toward home and my husband. We had traveled a lot together and only on a few occasions had I traveled alone. I wondered if he was missing me, too. My cell phone rang and I answered it. It was him! He called to confirm the time he would be at the airport to pick me up. As I listened to his voice, I knew he missed me and thought of how our thoughts had come together when he decided to call! It was a wonderful valida-tion of how we send and receive thoughts, and that our communication was manifested into the physical by his phone call! It felt almost magical to me.

As much as I was missing my husband and my home, I enjoyed being at Peace River, and being able to share it with Christine and my new friend, April, made it an extra special time.

The next morning, I could hear my 4 a.m. voices in the distance and I opened my eyes to see what time it was. Yes, it was 4:15 a.m., and for a minute I smiled and thought, "Wow, I am running late this morning!" And as I sat up looking at the suitcases, I wondered what next month was going to hold. I heard Friar greet me with "Good morning," and as I looked around, I could see the group of people in the room. There was Wayne, my dad, April's husband, and Christie's father-in-law, my grandmother, April's guide Sally, Christie's guide Charlie, and Friar. It felt like a full house! As I looked out over the river, I saw that it was as still as glass. I grabbed my headset and tape recorder and headed out onto the patio to do a meditation before everyone awoke.

The meditation was one where I envisioned entering a workplace and walking down a corridor. As I walked down the long hallway, I opened a door and, as I walked through it, I saw guides I knew as well as ones I didn't. When I asked who they were, a woman turned to me and put her finger to her lips in a gesture of "shhh," and pointed to me to leave. I went out the door and thought, "Hey, wait a minute; this is my workplace. Why can't I stay in there?" As I came out of the meditation a little irritated, I opened my eyes and saw Friar and Wayne smiling. I asked them why I wasn't allowed to stay in there, and Friar's reply was that "I wasn't ready, yet." He told me that when the time was right, all the guides would present themselves when they were needed. It was at this moment when I learned of the number thirty-six. Friar said that, although I may not know them all, I had thirty-six guides. He assured me that there would never be more and there would never be less than the thirty-six. He went on to say, "It is something that you did not need to worry about. You never have been nor ever will be alone."

Once again, the word "patience" was beginning to frustrate me. Every time I asked for more information, like "What does the thirty-six mean?" or "Can I get history on Friar?" or whenever I wanted to know more than they were willing to share with me, I would only see Friar step back. The more I pushed, the more he stepped back. It was frustrating for me, because I felt I was working very hard! Even Wayne would step back with Friar when I got into a mood where I wanted to "know" more.

LIFE *is a* CLASSROOM

*"To be on a path of discovery is like standing in a
seeded garden and being amazed at the beauty as the
flowers appear into full bloom."*

During the next three weeks, we practiced what we learned in
Sandy's classes every day. There was not a day that went by
that I didn't do my "homework" and work on making great
strides forward.

Jeff and I decided to have a garage sale one weekend. It
has become almost a ritual at our home to have garage sales
to clear out some of the stuff that we'd collected. I think
sometimes our home is a magnet for it.

We set the sale up in our driveway, with me sitting by the
table with cash box at hand, waiting for the people to pay for
their treasures. At one point, my husband backed a van into
the driveway, swung open the van's back door, and started to
pull out something. "Ah….what is this?" I thought. It was a
desk I had not seen before.

Suddenly, standing next to me was Jeff's mother, who had passed away in October, 2000. I heard her say, "You know, it would be nice if it was refinished." I couldn't help but ask Jeff if it had been his mother's desk. He said he thought so, since it came from his sister's house. I was now starting to share the information I received more openly with him. After Wayne's passing and prior to Sandy's classes, I was selectively silent about the information that was coming through. I didn't believe that other people in the physical world would have a positive reaction to hearing the information that I was hearing. But because of Wayne and his wife, Marian, Christie, Sandy and now Mic, I was stepping out of the cocoon I had placed myself in.

Sandy was becoming a very strong mentor in my life. I have often referred to her as my "Mother Hen" when talking about my experiences with her: she was just that! She knew how hard it was for me to step out when I really wanted to step back. Sandy encouraged me and when I didn't display faith in myself or my abilities, she pushed me out, front and center. She had strength in her classroom when dealing with the students: at times she could be gentle and sometimes she'd be "right in your face." I had a healthy respect for her ability as a mentor.

Sandy and I were keeping in touch through e-mail on a regular basis. After the sale, I told her that people from the other side attended the sale as well, and I told her about the comment from Jeff's mom. What Sandy said about Jeff's mother and the garage sale was priceless, and I use it often. Sandy said, "Life is a classroom, isn't it?" Boy, did she hit the nail on the head.

Soon after, Jeff and I decided to take a trip down to Peace River. He was interested in meeting Sandy and seeing what was going on down there. Could anyone blame him? I had set up an appointment with Jason Oliver for Jeff. Jeff's deceased mother had visited me during the last class and had continued to pop in every now and then. She said she would be there when Jeff and I went to Florida.

I felt really good about Jeff coming with me to see Peace River. We enjoyed the drive down from Tampa, and took in some local sights while we were there.

When we arrived at the store, I introduced Jeff to everyone. It was the store's monthly Psychic Fair Weekend. Jason came out of the room he was using for his readings and introduced himself. Jeff and Jason disappeared into the room together for the reading, and I just hung out around the store.

I spent the half hour roaming the store and taking in the sights. John was behind the counter scheduling appointments with the local psychics they used at the store. Sandy was busy behind the coffee counter and circulating around the store greeting customers.

When Jeff and Jason both returned, I asked Jeff if his Mother had come through. He replied, "No." Man, I could not believe that she didn't show up. I had believed her when she said she would. Jason came over to say goodbye and as he did, I told him that I was disappointed because someone hadn't appeared for Jeff. He said, "Jeff your mother is here; she waited until we were all together," and then he validated her presence by describing her appearance and what she was like in life! Jeff was surprised. I believe it was a huge valida-tion for Jeff. He was hearing from a stranger the information that validated that his mother was present. As I had shared with him, she promised she would be there. For me, I was relieved and pleased that it worked out for him and me!

Jeff met Sandy and saw the store. It was now something he could see in person and was able to picture where I was spending my time and who I was spending my time with. We enjoyed having the time together and away from home! I was elated that I was able to share Peace River with him.

When we arrived home, our Dalmatian, Josie, seemed sick. I got in contact with Sandy and asked her if she thought I could do a body scan on a dog, She replied, "Why not"? So one morning, when Josie was lying in on floor, I sat next to her and applied what I had learned. I placed my hands over her and visualized I was walking through her body. I started at her head and worked through her body. I asked my guides to please help me get the information I needed in order to help her. I then made an appointment with the vet.

Toward the end of the examination, I asked the doctor at the Shady Oak Veterinary Clinic if she would check Josie's thyroid! Dr. Barb had taken care of Josie since she was a puppy. She asked a few questions about the symptoms that Josie was presenting. I shared with her that she seemed to have less energy and I had the feeling that something was wrong with her thyroid. She offered to do a complete blood panel. I asked her if a specific thyroid test existed. Dr. Barb commented that it would cost extra, and that if anything was wrong, it should show in the blood panel screening. I insisted that she do the other test as well. The validation came when the blood panel test results looked normal, but the thyroid test revealed that she was hypothyroid.

This experience really validated the value of the skills I learned with Sandy. However, it is important to note, and Sandy was very clear in her teaching, that having a psychic give you a body scan does not replace visiting a doctor and getting a doctor's opinion. I am not a qualified physician, and I only offer information that I feel or am given. Often, having this information can be helpful for a person when he or she visits her physician, but it should never replace a qualified physician's report.

RESONATE TUNING *at* WORK

*"Compassion must first be given to self
so that we may freely share it with others."*

It was now time to plan for our August class, the third of the six classes that were part of Sandy's curriculum. April would not be attending due to a conflicting engagement, so Christine and I would be on our own. We decided to drive down to Florida with her three children and my niece, Mandy, who would care for the children while we were in class. We decided to go to Orlando to take the children to Disney World after our visit to Peace River. The Holiday Inn was now assigning the same room to me each time I stayed at Peace River. It had a great view and gave me the feeling of familiarity.

The topics in the upcoming class were automatic writing, crystal gazing, using a pendulum, psychometry, and past life recall. Next month would be the introductory mediumship class, or communicating with people on the other side.

Upon our arrival to the hotel, a young man that I usually saw working there checked us in. He was friendly and always kidded around with us. He was interested in what we were doing. We offered him a reading on Sunday night if he was interested, and he accepted. His name was Chad. This is what happened at Chad's reading.

Christine and I joined Chad out by the pool for the reading. We explained to him that we do not summon people who have died, and that the people around him may not be the folks he was hoping to hear from. We assured him, though, that they would be the ones he needed to hear from. We mentioned that we could be wrong in our interpretation of what the people meant, but we could not be mistaken in what we would see or hear. If, for example, I were to see someone on the other side wearing a train engineer's outfit, like Casey Jones', it could mean that the man worked on a train, or that he had a career as some sort of engineer, or both! And so we let Chad know that we would give him whatever information we received and allow him to interpret it.

The first person who came through was his paternal grandmother, followed by his maternal grandfather. They validated the upbringing of his dad and his mother. The grandparents then went on to explain that they knew about the conflicts that Chad had faced with his dad and they knew his preferences in life. We gave Chad information about what was coming up in his life. Even though he could validate the information we gave him, Chad seemed unsettled and sad at the close of the reading.

We asked him what was wrong, and he stated that he had hoped that one other person would come through. When I heard that, I asked if anyone else wanted to step forward and give Chad a message. A young girl came through. She had been killed in a car accident and shared with him that she was okay and that he needed to let go of the guilt about not being around prior to her death. She also told him who had been with her in the car. This validated our information.

She mentioned that Chad had driven by the scene of the car accident after it had happened, but had not realized that she had been in the car. She gave him information about her funeral and the yellow dress she wore. We even told him about the way she would put her hand on his knee when she was trying to get her point across to him when they were in deep conversation. Chad was happier now that she had come through, and we closed the reading.

The weekend class was full of surprises. We worked on meditations, and then moved onto the new adventures. We were introduced to psychometry, which is something I now really like to do. All the students put an object of some sort into envelopes and, upon sealing them, we placed them into a container. They were mixed up and everyone drew an envelope. With the envelopes sealed, we were asked to hold the object between our hands and give a reading about it.

The envelope I chose was thin and light. I held it between my hands and this is the information I received:

I felt the item in the envelope was related to someone who had problems with anger. I could feel it as it welled up inside of him. It was a young male who was experiencing bouts of depression, who perhaps even had to take antidepressants or seek other professional help. I felt that this person had a problem with family, something related to a divorce. He was very upset and felt a great loss. I felt that the person was tall and rather thin.

When I completed the short reading, I opened the envelope. It had contained a picture of a young man who was tall and thin. A woman in her late forties, generously built with colored, blonde hair, claimed the picture and said that I was way off-base. She was not depressed, didn't have anger issues, was not male, and was not tall and thin. She stated categorically that her divorce was in the past. "Boy, did I mess up," I thought. Sandy was quick to interject, asking, "Who is the picture of?" The woman said, "My son." Sandy explained that when you read a picture, you read who is in the picture and Sandy asked the woman if my reading fit him. The woman said, "He was getting psychological help because he was having trouble with the divorce. He was on antidepressants. He is tall and thin and has anger issues." Boy, was I surprised!

I discovered that psychometry is one of my favorite things to do! Christie and I spend a lot of time doing psychometry on a very regular basis.

We were now on to automatic writing and crystal gazing. We were told we would first do a meditation and that after the meditation, we would need the crystal we selected to use from the store, along with our tablet and ink pen. Once we completed the meditation, we were to first do the crystal gazing, and then write down what we saw. After the crystal gazing, we would do automatic writing. I thought this was really weird stuff, but thought that it would be fun to try it.

After the short meditation, I picked up the smokey quartz crystal I selected from the store. I gazed into the crystal until I saw what appeared to be a few silvery branches. They looked like branches in the winter time, when snow crystals shine on them, making them look silvery and shiny. I didn't see a scene or anything else, just the silvery branches.

The automatic writing proved to feel very strange. My arm seemed to take on a life of its own. The words it wrote down were, "Come join us, work will seem like play." I could hear a larger-than-life voice say the words, and as my hand

and the pen scrolled across the paper, I felt a little uncomfortable as I felt my arm float.

When everyone was done and it was time to share what we had received with the class, I felt embarrassed. I sat back and listened as students talked about wonderful scenes they had seen in their crystal reading. And as the students talked about their writings and how they were long and had lots of information, I thought to myself, "I'm probably going to disappoint Sandy on this one, because my message seems so small." As the students shared their stories one by one, I felt concern over what I had and how it wasn't looking very good!

Christie sat next to me with her paper in hand, and we both wished we had gotten the kind of information the other students had. Sandy, observant as always, let me sit through each student's report. Finally, with her eyes pinned on me, she walked over and said, "And Susan, what did you get?" I felt embarrassed as I shared with everyone that all I had gotten were some silver branches while I was crystal gazing and that the automatic writing resulted in only a few words. I read, "Come join us, work will seem like play." Sandy smiled and reassuringly stated, "Susan that is great. Sounds like you got a message directly from the White Brotherhood." Wishing I knew more about metaphysics, I had no idea what she was talking about nor did she explain what she meant.

After class, I asked Sandy what she meant by the White Brotherhood and she referred me to the works of Alice Bailey, telling me that Bailey refers to the masters, or the members of the White Brotherhood, in her books. I've since learned that among the masters Bailey discusses are Jesus and Buddha, and that all the masters are believed to have walked for a time on earth. It is said that all religions, including Christianity, Buddhism, and others, were based on their physical experiences. And, as far as the "work will feel like play" message… I now think that perhaps it describes my approach to my work.

I was raised Lutheran, and although I believe in the Father, Son and Holy Spirit, I can also look "outside of the box" in which we have categorized different religious experiences. I can recognize that just as Jesus taught love and devotion, each of the masters brought divine teachings as well. Of course, I am not wise enough to know which religion is correct. Perhaps all share in the divine presence we call God.

At Starchild that August day, Christie had drawn a map that closely resembled an area of New York known as Long Island. And during the crystal gazing, she saw a brown haired man. Sandy was impressed with the drawing of the map, but didn't give an explanation for it. She only commented that perhaps a brown haired man was coming into Christie's future for some reason. She did not expound on the topic.

I came away from this class feeling much more confident and knowing that I really wanted to work with psychometry. I shared with Christine that I felt crystal gazing was too slow, and it was too subjective for me.

Christie and I talked quite a bit about automatic writing. She liked it, while I didn't care for it. I just didn't see why you would sit and wait for your arm to write a message when you could hear the message directly from the person on the other side. Having to relinquish control of my arm was also something I disliked. I have a strong feeling about a spirit moving my arm and my reaction is NO THANK YOU. The other side can talk to me, I can sense what they feel, I can smell a fragrance, or see them, but my body is mine, thank you very much. These feelings have always been very strong, and I do not see them changing in this lifetime.

On that month's trip, I was able to have several sessions with Mic. Mic journeyed to the Holiday Inn and set up a healing space in our hotel room each of the five days we were there. It seemed like the theme of my healing sessions was learning to trust my feelings. He was working with both my guides and his, helping me learn to open the door to accepting and trusting the information that I was receiving.

It was a pivotal five days for me, and I released many of the old hurts that I was carrying. Even though the validations were presenting themselves all around me and my guides were working 24/7, I had doubted myself for so long that the hurdle I now needed to cross felt huge. In fact, it felt that self-doubt had taken up permanent residence in me. It was time for a change and Mic opened a door so that I could feel compassion for myself. The journey I began with Mic is one I am still pursuing today.

During the last healing of the weekend, I had a vision just as the session was coming to a close. I saw two hands above me, each with a dove perched on it. It was as vivid as you would see in your own hands. It gave me the feeling of eternal peace and comfort.

After we had packed up our things so that we'd be ready to leave Peace River the next morning, I was able to spend a few minutes before bed, sitting and looking out over the River, reflecting on the last five days. I thought of the three little boys bedded down in the room, and how blessed I was to be able to feed the sea gulls with them, and have them experience how freeing it felt to have the birds take flight about us. The children had giggled, and I could still see their smiles of pleasure as they gave the birds the bread they had broken for them. I wondered what change the moments we had here might have on the children, and then I saw Friar smile as if he was approving of what I was thinking.

I felt deep gratitude for being able to share this with my daughter and her children. Then my thoughts turned to my sons back home and their children, and I wondered if I would be able to share moments like these with them someday.

As I saw Friar's soft, warm eyes and his smile, I knew the comfort I felt was part of the deep gratitude I had for being on this journey and path of discovery, and from knowing that this was part of the journey of a lifetime. I felt complete for the first time in my life, and I knew that if I were to die the next day, I would be complete. My life was full of the song that made my heart sing.

For just a moment, sadness drifted over me. Looking at the view outside my room, I knew that there were so many people crossing the bridges that spanned Peace River who were still searching to find what would make their hearts truly sing.

the
TELEPHONE LINE

*"We are all connected and it is in God's presence
that our spirits are lifted and soar."*

It was now September, 2002, and time for the fourth class in the series of six. This was the P4 class of the Anastasi System of Psychic Development, or "Introduction to Mediumship and Channeling." P5 and P6 are all about mediumship and spirit communication.

On that month's Northwest Airline flight to Tampa, I was filled with anticipation. My mind drifted back to when I started the program with the first class, and how I had wished I were in the class that Jason had been teaching in the room next to Sandy's. Saturday would be the start of the next three months of spirit communication, where we'd study, among other things, receiving messages from the other side.

Learning why I could communicate with the other side was very important to me and, so far, the classes had provided me with hands-on experiences and validations that I truly valued. But I was looking forward to learning more, to being with Sandy, and learning what she had to teach.

I planned to arrive two days early so that I can spend time with Mic before the weekend class and to stay a couple of days after the weekend was over. I found that the work we were doing together helped me achieve balance and make better sense of the experiences I was going through as I moved through the series of classes with Sandy.

April and Christie would be arriving on Friday. Christie would have to return early Monday morning, and April's plans were to stay until Tuesday with me. She wanted some time to work with Mic, too.

Getting off the plane in Tampa, renting a car, and then driving across Tampa Bay felt almost routine by now and I found joy and comfort in seeing the sea gulls, pelicans, and beautiful surroundings welcome me to the west coast of Florida, inviting me to drive south.

My first stop was at the Holiday Inn. Mic was driving down to the hotel to do a healing session with me, and then we were going to dinner together.

As I had anticipated, this session with Mic helped me bring together and balance all the things I had been practicing over the month. This time, I experienced something new, though. As Mic worked with my energy, I began to really understand how he was doing what he was doing. I could actually see the energy patterns as they moved.

During the session, I also shared with him that his mother was standing next to him. He asked what she was saying, and I shared with him what I saw and heard. In life, his mother let me know, she had a deep affection for him that had caused him great pain in his relationship with his dad and brother. He confirmed that his father and brother resented him for the preferential treatment he received from her. I found it interesting that, when Mic worked on me, I also was receiving information about him.

Mic and I planned to work together for about a week each month. I looked forward to learning everything I could from him.

After the session, we went to dinner at a little Italian restaurant in Punta Gorda. He introduced me to my first cannoli. I loved the pastry with the whipped cheese filling and the chocolate chips.

Arriving back at the hotel, I realized that it was nice having a little time to myself before the girls arrived. I was able to pick up bread at the bread outlet store. The hotel room now had a microwave and refrigerator in it. On each trip, I would go to the Publix grocery store and pick up a few things for the time I would be spending at the hotel.

I had made arrangements for Mic to come to the hotel on Friday and Sunday night to work on all three of us. There wouldn't be enough time to get to Sarasota after the classes. Christie had made plans to return home first thing Monday morning, and we knew our time with her would be very limited.

The first day of class proved to be very interesting. We were introduced to channeling, and we did a meditation before starting the work.

We were asked to pick someone we hadn't worked with yet. As I felt a hand rest on my shoulder from behind, I thought, "Please, not the psychologist." Sure enough, I turned around and a gentleman in his late forties or early fifties was smiling at me and asking to partner up for the exercise.

Bob traveled from the northern east coast to Florida to take Sandy's class. We were asked to take five minutes to breathe and connect with our Higher Selves. We were preparing to give information to our partner that was not based on empathy or telepathy. Instead, we were instructed to channel information about the future. After a moment, I shared with Bob that he was investigating or reporting about something. I also felt that he was going to be doing mediumship as part of his business, and that he would excel at it. I can't remember the details of all the information I got, but I remember later that he confirmed that he was doing a paper on the topic. And today, a couple of years later, he actively does group readings and applies spirit communication to his practice.

His reading for me that day included seeing me on a stage in a huge building. I was doing readings similar to those that John Edward does, and I was doing this in a large auditorium. About a year later, I was on the stage of the Northrup Auditorium at the University of Minnesota, doing readings for a group of people. I found that when you channel futuristic information, the validation comes later. It is difficult for people to give you a yes when they aren't even aware that it is going to happen!

After lunch, the spirit communication part of the course was to start! I was probably the only one in the room willing to skip lunch that day. The class was being taught by Jason Oliver, Sandy Anastasi, and John Maerz.

During class, the instructors passed out handouts about mediumship. John Maerz had written one on what to expect when you bring dead relatives through from the other side. John made a statement about relatives in the physical and after they pass can be, "Stupid here, stupid there," and I was puzzled by these words. I now believe that he meant to say that a person doesn't instantaneously get smarter when he or she passes to the otherside. But at the time, I found John's words worrisome.

I had just spent the last three months working on thinking positively about my abilities and learning to manifest things in a positive way. From my perspective, John's comment did not fit. Why would I put that type of energy into communicating with the other side? I thought that it was strange that someone who was so studied and had so much knowledge would make a comment like that about dead relatives. I really found John's attitude offensive, and thought that it showed a lack of respect for those who had crossed over. After all, if we have the ability to grow here, don't we have the ability to grow there as well?

This was the first time I really had a negative reaction to what I was learning at Starchild.

Another handout had a diagram that students could use to help them identify the people from the other side who they might see or feel in their readings. The students were to feel the deceased person on their right or left, and then ask the person to back up one or two steps. In this way, the medium can determine the generation in which the deceased person belongs. For example, if the deceased person takes only one step back, he or she would be the mom, dad, aunt or uncle. If the deceased person takes two steps back, he or she would be the grandpa or grandma, or another member of the grandparents' generation. The medium could then interpret the information she was receiving more accurately.

This method did not resonate with me, because when I did a reading for someone, I always saw the relatives around that person, and not around me. I usually just observed, listened to, and felt the people from the other side, wherever they happened to show up. Personally, I didn't want to have the deceased person by me as I was doing a reading for someone else. The idea of this made me uncomfortable.

While waiting for my turn, I saw Jason stand and make faces as he scrutinized each student's work. The whole thing made me feel very uncomfortable, and I dreaded my turn.

But my turn came soon enough. I was asked to stand and face the teachers, shut my eyes, and feel the spirit pull me to whomever the reading was for. As I turned and faced the teachers, I shut my eyes. I could feel the spirit gently tug at me to turn, and so I did. When I turned and opened my eyes, I could see several spirits around each person. Jason asked, "Is the spirit to your right or left?" I asked him, "Whose?" I could feel his frustration with me as I saw him twist his mouth from side to side, clearly trying to understand what I meant by my response. It quite frankly scared me to death: I felt like a child being scrutinized by her teachers and peers.

Frustrated, Jason told me that he was asking about my right or left. I stood there looking at one of the students, thinking that I had to figure out how to ask the spirit next to her to come stand next to me. My mind was going a mile a minute. I thought, "Well, I could at least try to get her father to move to her right side. I know Jason wants me to have the spirit next to me, but I just can't do that." In my opinion, it only made sense that her father belonged with her, not with me. I stood there looking like Bambi in headlights; I felt I was in trouble. All I wanted to do was sit down. I turned and looked at Jason and said, "Jason, her right or mine? I cannot do this. May I sit down?"

As Jason's frustration grew, I heard Sandy's voice. She said, "Susan, just start over and feel the spirit pull you and then do it your way!" I felt instant relief. I had been ready to run out of the room, I was so frustrated and embarrassed. Sandy's remark lifted me up, and helped me be willing to do it. I did the reading this way: I turned around as I felt a spirit pull me, just as Jason wanted me to do. Then I looked at the woman whose father was the first spirit to get my attention. I shared with her that he was from a family of five. He was tall, dark-haired, and had a moustache. He died early of a heart attack. I shared with her that when he passed, he was greeted by his mother and father on the other side. It went well, and I felt in my own element doing the reading this way.

Sandy remarked to me some time later that she, too, prefers the spirits to be around the person getting the reading and not around her. Ditto! Sandy and John later changed their classes to teach students to see the deceased behind the client and to complete the reading this way.

By the end of my classes at Starchild, I was able to communicate with three, four, and even five spirits around a person, and give details and messages within a five minute timed period. And I saw the spirits the way I had always seen them growing up. I got information by listening and talking to them, and then I shared what I saw, heard and felt.

The class sessions gave me a lot of practice standing in front of a group and just relating what I saw, felt, and heard. My practice during class really sped up the time it took me to receive information, and I learned to discern the kind of information I now refer to as "markers."

I usually get a number right away from the person on the other side. I know now that this number tells me how many siblings are in the family. Next, I usually get information that refers to the family the person grew up in or the family that he or she started. Interestingly, I often receive information that includes facts about miscarriages and abortions. The other side is definitely aware of every soul in a family unit.

On Saturday, Jason Oliver was doing a "Messages from the Other Side" session, and Christie, April, and I decided to attend. We thought it would be fun to see him work and perhaps get a message from someone on the other side!

Though I didn't know it in advance, once again, I was going to learn another important lesson.

There were about twenty people sitting in a horseshoe, or gallery, seating arrangement. Jason went from one person to another, giving messages. As he progressed, I noticed that he kept bringing in grandmothers. I felt that the session was a little boring: everyone seemed to be hearing from a grandma. I knew there were many other spirits in the room, and was curious why he continuously chose to communicate with the grandma figures.

After the session, I went up to him and asked a question. Jason was one of the instructors for the mediumship classes, so I felt comfortable enough to pose a question to him, student to teacher. Unexpectedly, though, I tripped the "ego switch." I asked him, "Jason, if each person you were reading had more than one relative near them, would it be okay to choose to read someone other than the grandmother, so that there would have been more of a variety?" Jason snapped back, "Not every one is a John Edward and gets names and dates!" Oops, I just stepped on his toes! I hadn't meant to offend him: I just wanted to know the etiquette of reading, and how a medium should choose which spirit to read first!

Perhaps Jason felt stressed: after, all, he had taught all day and then had done twenty readings that evening. But his irritability carried into the next day. Jason started making jokes about Sagittarians. Considering that only two students, me and another student named Dale, were the only students with the astrological sun sign of Sagittarian, I knew exactly who the jokes were intended for.

After the Sunday class, I shared with Sandy that I didn't think I would be coming back: I was having difficulty with Jason's classroom antics. She explained that he was under a lot of pressure and was planning a move to Hawaii. She also said that he would not be teaching the next class because of his move. I was relieved but also sad. He had given my husband and me readings that meant so much to us. It was difficult to see another side of Jason.

Through my work with Mic, I was learning to recognize, many times reluctantly, that there were intricate parts of me that I needed to become aware of, to be open to, and to accept if I wanted to heal the wounds that were holding me back on my journey. In the space, that I felt diminished by Jason's antics helped me recognize the times I had diminished or could diminish someone else with my own behavior. I've learned that healing yourself can be very painful, especially when you see more about yourself than you saw before. But for me, healing always opened new possibilities that I could now recognize and that I couldn't see before. In my sessions with Mic, I didn't feel particularly brave for looking at the things that were blocking me from progressing, but I did feel pain. My growth truly showed when I chose to replace pain and self-judgment with compassion and the feeling of an opening of light.

Over the next few months, we took more classes in mediumship, and one of my favorite moments was when Christie got up to do a reading. Sandy was behind a video camera taping the class. Christine began her reading, and turned around as she felt the pull of spirit. When she opened her eyes, all she saw were two empty chairs. Behind the chairs was the camera and next to it was Sandy, checking the taping of the class. John Maerz and Ed Hicks were seated toward the front of the classroom, and were teaching with Sandy. They suggested that perhaps the person getting the reading was in the chair next to the empty chairs. Christine said, "No. I feel it belongs right here," and she pointed to the empty chairs. They had her repeat the steps, and when she did, she turned to the same position. They told her to go ahead and tell them what she could learn.

So going with it, she said, "I'm sensing both a female and male energy. They are one step back, so I think it makes them parents. I am getting a name like Mahogany and you come from a long line of spruce. I'm feeling pain in the midsection and am not sure how the parents passed. The message is that they know you really wanted to be a table, but being a chair is just as important and don't ever forget it." The class burst into hysterical laughter as everyone realized she was reading the wood chairs in front of her. Christie's acting ability was shining!

With all kidding aside, she then went into the reading of a person on the other side. The presence coming through was Sandy's grandmother. Sandy was behind the chairs! Christine stuck with the information she was getting about Sandy's grandmother and Sandy got a reading! This is not an easy thing for a student to do. The last thing most students want is to read one of their teachers. On breaks we often talked about how uncomfortable it could be to do a reading of our teachers. What if some information came through that embarrassed the teachers or revealed private information? I was really proud of my daughter for sticking with what she was getting!

In November, we had the last mediumship class. At the close of the weekend, all the students were going to gather at the Holiday Inn for a graduation party along with our teachers.

During the class that weekend, we had an exercise in reading what they called a "billet." We were told that the exercise was supposed to be fun and light-hearted. We were asked to write a question that we wanted a spirit from the other side to answer. We were handed a recipe card size piece of paper, were told to write down our questions, and then to fold the paper in half and place it in the box. The box would then be passed around, and each of us was to take one and then read it with out opening it, only by holding it in our hands and listening to spirit.

When it was my turn to stand up, I took a billet and read it. I stood there for a moment. I saw my brother, Wayne, on the other side laughing and saying hello. I turned to the teachers and said, "I cannot read this!" John asked, "Why not?" I replied, "Because it is my billet." John looked at me, smiling, and said, "Well, if it is yours, what is the answer?" I stood there for a moment and replied, "I see my brother laughing and he says hello!" I opened the billet and read the question. The question was, "Wayne, do you have a message for me?" Everyone started to laugh; it was a moment when I learned that you need the confidence to own what you feel is correct for you.

Then it was time for another new experience. Christie selected her billet. As she did, I looked at the red-haired female student across the room, and I could feel anger well up inside of me as our eyes met. All of a sudden, Christie was visibly upset; she said she felt suicide around this billet. She requested to go outside and clear her head. The class was excused for a break. April jumped up and ran outside to check on Christie. The student then came over to me, apologizing for what she wrote. I asked her, "Why would you write something that would be so upsetting, when this was supposed to be for fun?" I have no doubt she heard the protective anger in my voice as I turned to head outside to Christie. Chris said she was okay, but that she felt that a young person was going to attempt to commit suicide. The question had been about the student's son.

On my way inside, John stopped me and asked if Christie and I had always had such a strong connection. I had the feeling that it took the teachers by surprise. I hadn't been consciously aware of what had just happened, but I now recognized that the instant Christie touched the billet, I knew who had written it and that Christie was going to have an issue with it. I now see how extraordinary this might seem, but on the other hand, why would it be strange? Christie and I have always been very close; she is my daughter, after all.

When April read her billet, she got "Wisconsin" and the word "cheese." The question was, "Who shot JFK?" Most of the questions where light-hearted, and it was fun to experience playing like this in class.

Our graduation party proved to be full of surprises. Christie, April, and I had gotten together to plan and pick up most of the trimmings for the party. Mic sang and danced to the song "Forever Young." John Maerz shared his abilities in "Meditation in Motion" and Ed Hicks showed us the art of t'ai chi. It was a great evening; the students shared a dinner of pizza with all the extra fixings. The party lasted well past midnight, and we knew it was a farewell. It would probably be the last time that many of us would spend time together.

To this date, whenever I hear on the radio Rod Stewart singing "Forever Young," I think about how hard each of the students worked, the dedication that Sandy and Mic put into their work, and the fact that their work would always continue on in ours. I was very proud to be a part of the experience of the Class of 2002.

A
STAR SHINES

*"To do the work that makes your spirit soar and your heart
sing is a gift to self and when it is of service to others, it
enables you to shine like a star from the heavens."*

During my trips to Sarasota to visit Mic, I met his life partner
Patti Star. The day I met her, I was sitting at the kitchen table
with Mic and April, when she entered the room and joined
us at the table. Her hair was long, thick, and reddish in color.
She'd had a hard day at work, sharing with us that she was a
massage therapist who used essential oils. Mic used a special
essential oil blend called "Euphoria" that Patti made for his
work. I asked her if she would make an oil blend for me, one
that would help me with my spirit communication, and she
graciously agreed.

Patti brought out and placed on the table a couple of
quilted cases, about eight inches square, containing little
bottles of essential oils. There must have been at least eighty

different oils. I saw her look at the aura around me, and I knew she was sensing information that she would use to identify the oils she would then mix into my special blend. She pushed back her long hair as if to concentrate on the task at hand, and it was obvious that she was listening to her guides and doing her work psychically. I was amazed how she knew just which bottles to choose: it appeared so easy for her. I remember how I felt the first time she asked me to smell the oils she was mixing; it was as if she opened a channel between my head and heaven. It felt surreal, as if I were on a cloud drifting back into my body. She smiled and knew she had the right blend. When she completed filling the bottle, she labeled it, "Susan's Work Blend."

Mic hadn't told us very much about Patti's background, and Patti was more intent on listening rather than speaking. April was with me that day, and as I watched Patti make April's blend, I was amazed by the way she once again just picked up the bottles and started blending the fragrant oils. As April inhaled the oils that Patti mixed for her, I could see April light up with excitement. I was fascinated by what I was witnessing. Anyone could see the expression on April's face change. I also saw April's aura change. The areas around April's chest radiated green with pink running in it; her overall aura had more white and green around it, and the connection from her crown to the ground was a stream of light running from above her head, through her feet, and into the ground. April said it made her feel wonderful.

I realized at this moment that another door was opening for me to walk through. Patti's work with the oils intrigued me, and it wasn't long before I was on her massage table getting bodywork done.

She has an office in downtown Sarasota, and the first time I walked into her room for a massage, I immediately smelled the prominent fragrance of the oils. As I walked through the door, I could feel tears welling up; a song "Calling all Angels" was beginning to play and I knew that, once again, I was going to be blessed by one of those "aha" experiences!

The first session with Patti consisted of a full body massage. She used the essential oils as she worked. I made many new discoveries that day as she worked through the hour session. Patti uses certain oils on certain parts of the body when she detects that particular oils are needed to release, calm or energize. Her movements when she does this are as graceful as those of a ballet dancer.

During the session, I discovered that Patti was also able to pick up memories of past events that were stored throughout my body. She was working on an area of my body, and all of a sudden I could feel the literal pain of a sword under my rib cage. I felt that I was being pierced on my left side, below my ribs. Patti stated that she felt it had something to do with a past life, and that I had carried the wound with me through many lifetimes. At the time, I couldn't identify the particular lifetime during which I received the sword wound, but could feel the pain in my side as she worked different areas of my body. When the massage was over, I felt relieved, but the pain was still in the background: I could still sense it.

I found that for months afterwards, the pain in my side would rise whenever someone explained something that didn't resonate with me and I felt challenged as a result. I could feel the twinge in my side. It would subside as I allowed the information to pass by and not take ownership of it. I wondered what it was about, but couldn't fully understand what it meant.

Most of the time I worked individually with either Mic or Patti, but periodically I had a session with Patti and Mic together. During one of these sessions, we were able to permanently remove the feeling of that sword. Apparently, the past life issue had something to do with my standing up for myself and not bending to someone else's beliefs or issues. Once I discovered the root of the memory left in my body, I was able to heal it permanently. I have not felt this pain since.

I found the work with Patti fascinating. I was interested in the fact that she was able to pick up current or past events as she did her massage work and by the way she blended her oils by listening to her own guides.

It wasn't until Sandy's class and my experiences with Patti that I formed an opinion about past life experiences. I hadn't really given a lot of thought to past lives, but my experiences in Florida quickly convinced me that all of us have past lives. I had heard once that King James took out all mention of reincarnation from the bible, fearing that his subjects wouldn't do as well in this life if they knew they had a second chance.

Patti uses a technique that I refer to in my classes as "connecting your head and heart." This technique enables a person to connect the mind's ability to process information with the heart's ability to process feelings about this information. We teach our students to do this exercise while breathing deeply. With practice, this exercise helps people connect their feelings with their intellectual insights, so that they act on a synthesis of both rather than merely from one or the other. I have found that it is better to spend some time in silence, processing your feelings and information. Afterward, you can speak from a place that truly represents you. This is helpful, especially when you want to share something difficult with someone. Learning this technique teaches us that we can act from a place of better understanding when we bring the head and heart together.

Patti offered a tremendous amount of wisdom and compassion as we worked together, and we became friends. She taught me just how important it is to stand for your truth and become empowered. Patti's ability to work with both past and present life issues is an amazing gift. I learned from her to encourage others to discover the benefits of aromatherapy, to become self-aware, and to gain the motivation to sit in the driver's seat.

Patti has a very multi faceted background, and holds a BA in psychology from San Jose University in California. Patti also holds a degree in aromatherapy and is licensed to practice massage in Florida and New York. She is also certified to teach t'ai chi, and to practice reiki and energy therapy healing. She had been practicing the art of aromatherapy for twelve years and had taught aromatherapy for the last six. She is a member of the National Association for Holistic Aromatherapy (NAHA), and served as the director for the west coast of the Florida branch. Patti is founder and owner of the School of Essential Oils Studies in Sarasota, Florida.

Patti enhanced all that I learned from Mic during my Florida experience. Mic was an essential part of the process of healing for me. Patti's work took my healing a step further by getting to the root of problematic issues in my life and work. I think of myself as a work in progress as I journey through this life, and I always look forward to spending time in Florida bringing balance and healing into my life and spending time with people who are close to my heart.

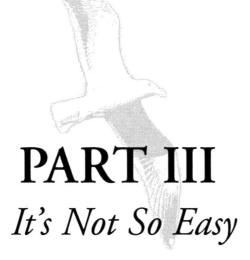

PART III
It's Not So Easy

CLASSROOM
in the SKY

*"It is through faith that man envisions the possibilities
that he manifests into his reality."*

All of the flying I did to and from Florida made for a lot of
time spent on planes. The flights usually lasted around three
hours, and they usually had quite a mix of people on them.

On one of my flights home, I had to stand in a line
waiting to use the bathroom facility. On this particular flight,
there were about eight people waiting ahead of me. I was
feeling a little anxious for some reason as I stood in line. That
anxious feeling usually is a strong clue, like a "heads up," that
I am about to discover something that might be a bit
challenging for me. The line was down to about five people
when I noticed a young man standing to the side of the
bathroom doors. He seemed to be talking to each person as
they approached their turn. I asked Friar what this was all
about, and all I heard was "Patience."

I knew that I was feeling anxious, and given that Friar said that challenging word again, I knew that the young man was going to be more than just someone saying hello to people. As I stood there with only one person in front of me, I heard him talk to the woman in front of me, though I didn't hear what they said. When the door swung open, she bolted into the bathroom; clearly, she was not happy with this young man and the conversation. I was now next and, as I stepped forward, I felt annoyed. The young man was tall and lean and had a determined stance. As I gazed into his eyes, I thought, "Oh dear, a born-again Christian on a mission." He smiled with a wide smile and said, "And, Ma'am, what do you do for a living?" I smiled at him and stated, "You don't want to know!" He said, "Sure I do." After we repeated this exchange a few times, finally I stated, "Look sir, please leave me alone." He said, "I just want to know what you do?" I thought, "Okay, Mister. You want to go there," and I decided to use the line that usually causes people to back off right away and leave me alone. With an edge of annoyance in my voice, I said, "I talk to dead people." His mouth dropped open, and he hesitated for a moment. But, do you think it stopped him? Not a chance. He said, "Ma'am, you shouldn't pray to the dead."

My instant come back was, "Why not, you do! Jesus died didn't he?" He stopped for a moment, and then said, "I mean, you shouldn't pray to dead relatives." I replied, "I don't. I just talk to them." It was now my turn to use the bathroom, and I was more than happy to get away from that young man. When I returned, he was enlisting others in a conversation about the art of praying and how I shouldn't be talking to dead people.

I took from this experience the idea that, if you feel that something is true for you and important to you, you can choose to hold on to it as yours. But debating with people who are close-minded is fruitless. Doing so doesn't resolve the debate but only adds energy to the debate.

On a different flight when I was returning from Florida, I heard Friar say, "Take notice; it's a minister." Over the past months I had wanted to discuss theology with a minister. So I thought that this might be just the opportunity I was looking for. I sat quietly in my seat, working on the computer, when a gentleman and his wife walked by and sat a row back on the other side. Halfway through the flight, I felt a hand on my shoulder. I looked up and the gentleman smiled and sat down next to me. I thought, "Wow. I need to be careful what I wish for. Now what do I do?"

The gentleman sitting next to me spoke softly, asking, "Do you mind if I sit here for a moment? I have a question for you." I thought, "For me?" He went on to explain that he and his wife had been sitting observing me as I wrote, and noticed that I would pause, and appear to be listening to someone or something. Then my fingers would start typing for a while and then I would stop and listen for awhile, and then repeat the whole thing over again. He said, "I just had to come over here and ask you a question: do you listen to guidance?"

I must have looked a bit startled by the question, but replied, "Yes, I do." I then asked him, "Sir, aren't you a minister?"

His replied, "Yes, but I am retired. My wife and I are on the way to Sioux Falls, South Dakota, to see our son who is now a minister at the church where I once worked."

I then mentioned that I had been hoping to meet a pastor who was open to psychic mediumship as well as theology. I was afraid of the repercussions if I talked to one of the pastors at my own church. I shared with him the story of my journey, starting from the time my brother passed away and ending where I was at the moment. I mentioned that I had a lot of questions about the Trinity of the Father, Son, and Holy Spirit. I also wanted to know what someone of his background thought about the possibility that perhaps masters other than Jesus walked under God. I was exploring the possibilities of viewing Jesus, Buddha, and other masters as a collective. He commented that he did believe in those possibilities. He gave me a name of a pastor in a suburb of Minneapolis who I could look up if I wanted to discuss this further. He thought that she would be interested.

I feel it was a gift of guidance that this man came into my life at that particular moment and shared his perceptions with me. That this happened as I was writing validated for me that a person from the Church could be open to the work I was doing and might understand all the possibilities I saw. I had met with so much disapproval from my family that having this kind and sensitive gentleman approach and talk was more than I could have hoped for.

I've often wondered why people assume that psychics and psychic mediums are not people of faith. If God created us in his likeness, why do people feel they need to remain small and not stand tall in his light and shine? It does not serve anyone to stay small. I find it interesting that I am Lutheran and yet feel comfortable discovering all the ways that God is manifested. The readings, teaching, and other work I do only strengthens my faith. And for all the people whose lives Christine and I have touched, it is more than believing… it is a "knowing"!

INTROSPECT...
A LOOK WITHIN

"To have courage to act on a vision
is like turning on a light
that enables you to walk a path of choice."

Christie and I were well into the psychic development classes when we kept getting clearer visions of some things we had seen previously, things related to our future work as psychic mediums. We found it difficult, though, to know if what we were seeing was just what we desired, or if it was some wisdom and information from the other side. When we first started our training, it was easy to interpret information that was about our own lives, since we didn't really have any expectations. But now that we were intending to continue working with our psychic abilities, we were finding it more difficult to distinguish between true messages and our own desires.

I've learned that one of the hardest things for a psychic to do is receive information about him or herself. This is the very reason psychics go to other psychics for readings! My experience has also taught me that it is best for me to go to someone who does not have a personal stake in my life. Otherwise, it can be difficult for that person to give an accurate reading. It is so much easier to do a reading for strangers than it is to do a reading for a family member.

Although Christie and I hadn't discussed anything with Sandy, we had been seeing the opportunity for Starchild to grow and change, and for us to be involved in that change. We knew that we were connected to this change in some way, but we didn't know exactly how or when. We just knew that we were located in Minneapolis and Starchild was in Florida. Any collaboration would involve a tremendous amount of traveling.

The visions we saw showed only part of a bigger picture. We saw ourselves perhaps participating in different events that would draw positive attention, bringing information to more students, and perhaps teaching classes nationwide. We saw many other options flash by. Because we have free will, we can respond to the guidance that we receive from the other side by choosing among the options that the guides present to us. The guides only present possibilities. It is my belief that a life guide will *never* make a person do anything that he or she does not want to do. Guides present choices, and it is up to us to choose what to do. Guidance is just that, guidance, and guides are there to offer you advice or counseling when you choose to listen. But they will not choose for you! When I hear a person say "My guide made me do it," I wonder who he or she is listening to!!! It's a red flag, and an indication that something is not right!

Christine and I had many discussions about what we wanted to do after the classes ended in November, 2002. We talked about our interests and our different options. We had similar interests and we both liked doing psychic readings and being mediums, though her preference was to work with children while mine was to work with adults.

Our confidence in our abilities to do this work had grown. By this point, I could not imagine doing anything else. I had found my element and I was tuned into the song my heart was singing.

We kept hearing that Sandy's store needed more business. Christine and I discussed possible ways that we could help them advertise. Sandy and John were very private about their personal lives, and understandably so. As a group of psychic students, many of us had already sensed the discord between John and Sandy and knew there was something wrong in their relationship. About six months after our graduation, Christie and I learned that they were divorcing but remaining business partners.

We knew we would need to establish our own company and company name if we were going to build a business and continue together on this path. The name would have to be special, and one day, while we were discussing the possibilities, Christie asked how I felt about the name Introspect. She had heard the word from Charlie, her life guide. We looked up the word "introspective" and found that it meant "taking a look within." It was a perfect name for the company and it was the beginning of Introspect...A Look Within. Given the work we saw ourselves doing, the name seemed very fitting. Christie and I had long discussions about starting this company. She is the one with the business mind, and so it was entirely appropriate that it started by her finding the perfect name.

My daughter's middle child, Josh, who was four at the time, gave us the final clue for the logo. I was sitting in the car with Christine and her children. Josh has a good heart.

Like many four-year-olds who want to own their own power, he said something to my daughter that sounded disrespectful. I asked him to sit back and think about what he had just said. After he calmed down, I asked him if he was sorry and his simple reply to me was, "Do you see a tear in my eye?" My reply was, "I should." And the image of his eye became the key element in our business's logo.

The business developed as we did readings for clients and later led to classes and events. Because of what Sandy, Mic, Patti, and April had done to help us develop and grow personally, we were hoping to have a relationship with them. We hoped that they could benefit from our work and perhaps advertise their own businesses. We had seen that all the businesses would remain separate entities, but that we would help each other along the way. After all, that is what the journey had been all about. And I truly wanted to help them as Christie and I helped our own business grow.

It was close to our graduation in November when I shared with Sandy what we had been seeing. I told her I saw the possibility of her company growing. We saw ourselves doing events, seminars and readings, both locally and nationwide.

We looked forward to the coming year with great anticipation. Sandy and I had become friends and I had planned to act on the visions Christine and I saw.

STRANGER *than* FICTION

"Some of the best moments in life are the ones we allow ourselves to see through a window of possibilities."

Within nineteen months of my brother's passing in April, 2002, I was licensed to do psychic readings in Florida. We were reading in several states, including Minnesota, Texas, Alabama, Colorado, Georgia, Louisiana, New York, and California. Christie and I were doing private readings as well as gallery style readings. We even did a large on-stage event.

We had been on several different radio shows and developed a curriculum that we still use to teach self-motivation and extra-sensory or psychic development.

Given the fact that we had been actively developing our skills for less than two years, these are massive accomplishments We often wondered where it all was going, but we enjoyed our work so much that it felt like play. The bonus in all of this for me is that I had the opportunity to work with my daughter, Christine, and to travel and do what really makes my heart sing.

Ruth Koscielak is one of the most well known female broadcasting personalities in the upper Midwest, with more than twenty years experience hosting midday talk shows. She currently distributes her show to stations around Minnesota through RBN Productions.

Ruth's guests often include newsmakers, celebrities, and well-known authors. And it was on her show that we first appeared on radio in the fall of 2003. She has been our favorite radio host; her candor and genuine warmth, along with her wit, always makes for an interesting listening experience.

When Christie and I first talked about going on the radio, I was rather hesitant about the idea of doing readings over the air. There was no time for us to practice doing this, we'd either get it right, or get it wrong. Christine contacted Sandy for advice, and Sandy thought that there was no reason I couldn't do it. My reluctance was just my insecurities getting in the way. When Christine shared that with me, I knew exactly what Sandy meant. But I won't say that I wasn't a bit scared.

We were also planning a large event where Christie and I would be on stage doing readings. We were planning on bringing in Sandy, Mic, and others for the event as well. Christine thought it would be great advertising to go on the air and do readings, and so, with a lot of encouragement, we contacted Ruth's office and before we knew it, a time was set for us to be on her show and we would be reading people calling in to Ruth's show for an hour.

The first time we appeared on Ruth's radio show, I was very nervous getting to the station. But Ruth was outgoing and friendly and the instant I put on the headset, all fears and worries were gone. We just took calls and gave the callers readings. The people calling in validated each reading and it went wonderfully and smoothly. I was relieved.

I find it funny that, even to this day, I still get very nervous just prior to appearing on Ruth's, or any other, show. But just as it went with my first appearance, the minute the headset goes on, I am in my element. Christie and I usually read together, and we have enjoyed each segment we have done. We have since spoken on many radio stations and inevitably the callers light up the phone boards and the call lights stay lit until we are out of the studio.

Christine and I were on the *Ruth Koscielak Show* during the Minnesota State Fair. We were in a small booth where fair-goers could to step up to a microphone and get a reading or ask a question. After several readings, a young woman stepped up to the microphone to ask, "Does my Dad try to communicate with me and is he turning the lights on and off in my house?"

My reply was, "Yes, your dad communicates with you. However, I know you want to believe that he is turning on and off the lights, but I do not feel he is. I see him sending you something that mesmerized you as a child; beautifully painted, winged insects. Do you know what I mean?"

Ruth spoke up as the woman just stood there. Ruth said, "Butterflies!" The woman bolted from the microphone and left before anyone could say anything else. Just then, a huge butterfly flitted into the area and sat on the book that a man who had been sitting next to her was holding. The audience gasped! For many, it was a wonderful validation. I hope the woman heard about it.

Validations are so important in our life. As humans, we look for validations from our parents, our spouses, and our peers. Children look to their parents to say "Job well done!" or "I am proud of you." High schools and universities use diplomas and graduation days to validate their students' achievements. Eulogies at funerals validate the value of life of the deceased for the survivors who are there to remember.

People look for validation that their loved ones are still around after death and that love transcends death. It is human nature to want validation, and as for the woman at the state fair and for many others, we need to be open to the possibilities that they are there for us! You don't need a medium to give you those validations, because such signs are in your life everyday. A medium can bring witness to your life and the deceased person's life. I feel the best validation of the connection between you and a loved one who has crossed over is when you feel the connection yourself, and you take ownership of it!

I was doing a reading for woman who had called in on the radio and later booked a private appointment. The woman's deceased husband was the first person to come in. I shared with her his physical description and cause of death. He let me know that he left her okay financially, and that she has a tendency to help their daughter too much. He went on to share that he knew his wife wasn't happy in her present relationship, and that he understood how much she missed him. He also shared that she was interested in another man besides the one she was having a relationship with. The wife confirmed the information.

He also told me that she was going to Florida. The wife confirmed she was due to go there on vacation. I then went on to give her a message. I said, "He says to watch the sunsets because they have the most beautiful sunsets there." I then asked her where she was going to be, and she said, "Disney." I thought that her response was strange, as I thought that she would be going to the coast, but I figured the truth would show itself in due time.

There was more to her reading but I mention just this part for a reason. I later learned that, during her trip to Florida, she was sitting at the center of Disney World when a man came up to her and asked her if she was from Minnesota. She replied that she was. He then remarked that he used to live in Minnesota, too, but that the Minnesota winters were too cold for him now. He then told her that she was sitting in a place where she'd see the most beautiful sunset in Florida! Then the man just walked away.

The woman called us upon her return home and tried to book an appointment just so she could share the story with me. I find this story particularly interesting because this husband's love and concern for this women and their family clearly transcends death. The deceased husband was aware of her trip with her daughter and grandchild and he knew where she was going to be and gave the validation ahead of time that he was going to get a message directly to her. The women had been depressed because of the loss of her husband. It was as if heaven shone a light on her face when she told me about her trip and the message she received. There was no sadness only joy, all because of the validation she received by feeling the connection she had with her husband.

Once, I was in Florida doing a reading for a woman who had quite a few relatives coming through. When Jason, her nephew, stepped forward, he gave information about a car accident. He clearly stated that he had not been driving and, as he stood in front of me, he showed me the color yellow. When a spirit does something like this, he generally has me see a thick cloud of color. I saw an injury to his head and chest, but I saw blood all around, as if he was physically traumatized in many areas. I could see things flying around in the car. He then went on to show me a scene of a lake and people fishing. He stated that his Dad had health issues going on. He showed me a brown colored garage and I saw bricks lined up that took the shape of a fireplace. I could see a young woman sitting at the cemetery who feels responsible for his death and said that healing needs to happen for her. He mentions his mother next by spelling out her name by holding up flash cards, one at a time. They spelled "A.... D.....A."

The women talked to Jason's parents and they validated all of the information that she learned during her reading. Jason's mother's name is Ada, his girlfriend was driving the car when the accident occurred, they were not wearing seat belts and were tossed around in the car. She survived the accident and feels responsible. The house they lived in had a brown garage, a brick fireplace, and the parents validated the importance of the color yellow and the fact that Jason's father was having health issues at the time.

While in Austin, Texas, I did a reading for a lady whose grandmother came through. The highlight of the reading was when her grandmother showed me a small notebook that flipped open over the top. I could see her sitting and writing something in it and closing it, only to open it again. She repeated this scene several times. Grandma was very intent about this notebook, and it clearly was of importance to her. I shared all this information with the woman, and she turned red in the face. Looking rather embarrassed, she said that she could not believe that Grandma was willing to share that information, but that Grandma was doing what she enjoyed doing when she was alive in New York, namely "running numbers" or betting.

This is a perfect example of how a medium does not always know what the person on the other side is communicating. By sharing what I saw and not trying to interpret it, the woman got a huge validation from her grandmother. It was something that her grandma really enjoyed doing, and the client could then unmistakably identify that it was her grandmother coming through. In this kind of situation, I act as a kind of gatekeeper and ask and receive help from my guides. If the woman really hadn't wanted to share the information with the others in the room, she could have chosen just to validate that she knew what it meant. Happily for us, she chose to liven up the room with the quip about her grandmother's gambling.

Christine and I were providing readings to a group of people in Minneapolis during a "Psychic Weekend" at a hotel by the Mall of America. It was to be a weekend of readings by Christine, April, and me. Mic was coming to Minneapolis to do healing sessions. We were doing private readings as well as holding a gallery reading session.

In the gallery session, I approached a woman sitting to the right side of me; her father from the other side was showing himself sitting by a desk with an old-fashioned adding machine, and was wearing an old-fashioned accountant's visor. He looked intent on running the machine and I could hear the numbers crunching. I shared with her the description of her father's physical appearance and the scene that I saw. I asked her why he would be doing that. She said she had no idea.

I continued the reading, and he kept going back to sitting at that desk, running those figures. I asked her again why he was doing that. This time, when she said she didn't know, her son, who was sitting in the back of the room, stood up and said, "Mom, I think Grandpa is worried about you spending the inheritance so fast!" It was a wonderful moment in which everyone got to witness the way a spirit can come through with a message of concern for their loved-one's welfare.

In another reading during the same session, I faced a different woman in the audience. The woman had dog after dog come in from the other side. After describing four or five dogs, including a dog that had allergies, I asked her, "Why do you have so many dogs coming in from the other side?" She smiled and replied, "I work for a county animal rescue organization and we rescue dogs for adoption!" The woman shared with us that she has always had a number of dogs of her own in her home, as well.

Another time we were in Dallas doing private readings at the Ramada Hotel. A finely dressed woman approaches me for a scheduled reading. Her husband appeared soon after we started. I gave her his physical description and cause of death, and although she validated what I told her, she didn't seem pleased about being there for a reading. I asked her why, and she said that she was there only because her sister dragged her along. I told her that I saw her husband rolling racks of plaid shirts across the room, and she looked shocked.

"Both of us hated plaid. I don't know why he would be doing that," she exclaimed.

He kept rolling rack after rack of plaid shirts across the room. I asked her what he did for a living, and she replied that he'd had a dry cleaning business. Well, that explained the rolling racks. I asked her if he had a hard time getting her attention. She said "Yes." I told her that I felt the plaid shirts were his way of getting her attention.

When someone comes through from the other side, much of what they reveal is about their unique perceptions of us, and their ability to see us and our lives from a different perspective. This kind of objectivity can be very useful, especially if we want to make changes in our lives.

During another reading for a woman from Dallas, a deceased husband came in wearing a train engineer's outfit.

She had no idea why he would be dressed that way and she wasn't willing to validate anything at the moment. Later in the reading, when she relaxed and recognized that other things I was telling her were true, she remarked, "Oh, you know… he was a chemical engineer and he did work on a railroad to put himself through college!" I find it intriguing how the other side often makes one thing mean several!

During a phone reading, I brought in the brother of a lady who lived in Florida. He shared information about his hospital stay and his death, but when I asked him about his burial, he seemed confused. He wouldn't share with me where he was buried and this made me feel that he was in limbo regarding his funeral. When I kept receiving a sense of confusion around his burial, I finally asked the client what he was talking about. Her reply was that he had just died forty-eight hours earlier, and they didn't know what they were going to do with the body yet! This helped, and I told the woman that her brother didn't really care, but that he wanted her to be mindful of his daughter's wishes and to stay close to his daughter, as she would need the support of her family in the near future! The woman confirmed that her brother did have a daughter and that she lived out of state. I guess they were trying to decide whether to ship his body out to his daughter who lived on the west coast, or bury him in Florida.

Once, when I was back in Port Charlotte, Florida, two very nervous women entered my hotel room for a reading that they had scheduled with me. They were referrals. I had never met them and knew nothing about them. Upon meeting them, though, I knew that they were mother and daughter. They were referred by someone I knew and upon introductions they shared with me that they had never had a reading.

I first read the mother, who was in her fifties and was tall and thin with brown hair. I explained there was a female energy around her that identified herself as Mother. The woman nodded to confirm that her mother had passed away. I mentioned that I felt she was about 5'7" and slender. She nodded yes again. I then went on to mention that she liked bright colors, especially red. She affirmed, again. I then went on to say I could feel a tightness in my chest, as if there was an unresolved issue around the two of them that needed clearing up.

I then heard the answers and told the woman, "Your Mother wants you to know that she chose to pass away after you had gone home. She states that she felt she couldn't pass while you were there, because she felt like she couldn't leave; she felt tied to this plane. Passing after you left was clearly your mother's way of making it easier on her and she felt it was easier for you, also. She expresses that she is sorry that you have felt so guilty for something that you had no control over, but that she gives you her warmth and love.

It is interesting that many people near death pass away when their family is away. I believe for some, it is because they need privacy or need to be separated from those they love in order to leave. I find this very interesting, given that my father died when the family members were all present. In fact, in his case, it was as if he waited for everyone to be there.

During that reading in Port Charlotte, I had more information to tell the woman. I said, "Your mom is showing me the pajama parties you used to have when you were in school. She says that the music was very loud at times. She tells me she had to go in to quiet you girls down." The woman's eyes welled up with tears. I went on to say, "The dreams you are having about your mother are really visits from her, and I encourage you to journal about them. She has been helping you with issues you have been having."

I then went on to describe the next person coming who came through. "He is about 5'9" and he is your father," I said. She confirmed this description. I went on to mention that he was on the larger side, but not fat, just broad in the shoulders. She confirmed this. I told her that he mentioned that he died from a sudden heart attack, and once again, she confirmed the information.

I went on to mention that he is more boisterous than Mother, and that he was the one who always sent Mom in to take care of the kids when they were "out of line." I then told her that I saw him gathering her mother up in his arms for a big hug, and says that the number five is very important. I think this was the number of kids and grandkids. I also told the woman, "He tells me the month of January belongs to Mom." She confirmed that it was her birthday month. I then explained that they were pulling back.

It was now the younger woman's turn. I mentioned that I saw four contemporaries that had crossed over; one was female and three were male. She confirmed. I then explained that they were together because they all died of alcohol-related accidents. She confirmed. The tall boy was nineteen or twenty, and he showed me a blue car that he got sick in. She confirmed that he vomited in her car. I then went on to say that this young man was taking responsibility for his death, because he ran into a tree while he was drunk. She confirmed that she was really angry with him. I then delivered the message, "Your friend says you need to let go of the anger, because he did what he felt he needed to do and it helped you out of a cycle that would have led you down a similar path of destruction." She said it was his accident that made her quit drinking. The message I gave this young woman that day was life-altering.

I then went on to say, "I see Grandma showing me a black dog. I also see Grandma showing me a baby girl and Grandma says this is your little girl here, alive. Grandma states that you were proud, because Grandma knew this little girl baby before Grandma died." The client confirmed that she had a black dog. She went on to remark that, as her illness progressed, her grandmother had a hard time recognizing people, but that she had still been able to recognize her baby girl. It was now time to close the reading, and I offered gratitude to the spirits for coming through.

Some spirits have the ability to communicate clearer than do others. I think it is like people here. We communicate more easily with the ones we are most attracted to. I have yet to meet someone who doesn't have a spirit around him or her, but I am aware that someday I may meet a person who doesn't.

This reading with the mother and daughter also demonstrates that I often see babies on the other side. I usually see those who have passed, and I've learned that it doesn't matter how they passed; they may have been miscarried, stillborn, aborted or perhaps they died in infancy. No matter the cause of death, they come through as a counted member of the family. It is my belief that souls come into the physical plane because they choose to and perhaps death is just the completion of their path, even for babies and children. People are very emotional when it comes to babies and children. I do not believe that a baby that is aborted or miscarried had no purpose and is merely a victim. I have seen the profound emotional reaction of a mother when her baby comes through, and I KNOW that, whatever the circumstances surrounding the baby's passing, the connection between baby and mother was important to both.

One time in Florida, I was planning on staying overnight with April at her friend Susie's house before flying home out of Tampa. I had not scheduled a reading with Susie, but her deceased mother was hanging around the house and April asked Susie if she wanted a reading before I left the next morning.

Susie lived in a northwest suburb of Tampa, Florida. The first person to come through was a woman wearing glasses who was about 5'6" tall. She introduced herself as Susie's mother and gave me the number three. The number three should have referred to the number of siblings or the number of children she had. The client validated that all the information was correct. I explained that Susie got her looks and mannerisms from her mom and that her mother and grandmother looked a lot alike as well. Her mother was noted for being the "hostess." Susie validated all information again.

The reading went on and her mother came in very clearly. I told Susie, "Your mother says she liked to "play it safe." She is standing beside your father, who has also crossed over. There is a man standing between your mom and dad. Your mom states that she married your dad only to find out later that the other man had wanted to marry her. She said she shared her life's story with you, so none of this should be a surprise.

Next, her mother mentioned a man named Ken, who was still alive. Your mother says, "that you have chosen to play it safe! She says that perhaps it is time to continue the platonic friendship you had with him." Susie's mother also said that she was sorry for interfering.

I then mentioned that I saw four generations of females with similar characteristics; they were all frugal, hiding money for a rainy day, and were the social hostesses of the family. They all played it safe in relationships by picking emotionally unavailable men. The women had married husbands with gambling and alcohol issues.

Susie's mother then went on to talk about the three children, and I also saw a baby with her on the other side. Susie confirmed that she had two siblings, and that her mother had had an abortion.

Susie's mom let me know that she was most concerned about issues concerning Susie's sister. I got the name Bobbie, and Susie confirmed that Bobbie was her sister's name. I told Susie, "I see a big wave in the ocean" and I went on to explain that I felt it meant her sister left a big mess after her passing. I said I felt she committed suicide and mentioned that her sister's life had spun out of control. Bobbie, it seems, was in such a dysfunctional state that she felt it was her only way out. I told Susie that Bobby died alone in her house. I also mentioned that I saw Bobbie gambling.

Bobbie then came in and stated that gambling had given her the illusion that her life was okay, but that her health had been deteriorating. Bobbie then said, "Susie shouldn't feel responsible because I wasn't found in time, and there is nothing she could have done to save me." Bobbie told me that it was her mother who had found her.

Susie validated everything, and I went on to share that I felt Bobbie was fine. In fact, Bobbie's presence felt very calm and she let me know that Susie had to let go of her death and stop thinking about what could have been or should have been. In Bobbie's opinion, Susie's concern about Bobbie's death was a diversion so that Susie didn't have to deal with her own life. Bobbie then went on to say how much she loved Susie and was grateful for all of Susie's concern and devotion. She hoped that Susie would remember them growing up and all the good times they spent together and let go of the end.

I then turned back to Susie's mother and father. Her mother asked, "Do you see the parallels in our lives?" and Susie's reply was "NO!" I explained that her mother was referring to the other man that was the love of her life, but who was thought to be gay. Susie's mother had married Susie's father, but had continued to love the other man from a distance. Susie now saw the parallel. Her mother said she was sorry for disapproving of the love of Susie's life and that perhaps it was time for Susie to rekindle that relationship. She told her daughter that it was time to put her energy into making her life better. Susie told me that, in fact, she had scheduled a visit with the "love of her life." He would be visiting her for Christmas. Some time later, she let me know that they were planning to go on a cruise together.

I did another reading for a woman named Holly, and it is a good example of how spirits use what I call "our file cabinet." Many times people on the other side use symbols, in this case prison bars, to communicate. An image can often mean more than one thing. After all, "a picture is worth a thousand words." We have what I call "a file cabinet" for a memory. And the image of prison bars is one item in my file cabinet. I used to watch the television show the Andy Griffith Show when I was younger. The character Otis was always locking himself in a cell after he had been out drinking. The jail house appeared frequently in the show. The day I did my reading for Holly, the other side decided to use my memory of this for a symbol.

The first person to come through was the grandma on Holly's father's side. I saw three men standing beside her. The first one was standing shoulder-to-shoulder with the other man, but was turned to the side. A third man hid behind them. In fact, it took a few minutes for me to see him. The man facing to the side wore earth-tone colors, his shirt was tucked in and he wore a belt. He was a little pudgy and had wavy, thinning, light hair. The man beside Grandma was heavier and had thinning hair the color of salt and pepper.

Grandma wore a high-necked dress with collar, and had on an apron that tied in the back. She wore rolled up hose and tied shoes. She was sweeping with a broom.

The man facing to the side was Grandfather. He showed me a scene of him behind prison bars, and gave me the feeling of being trapped in a situation. The man hidden would not move forward, and I felt that he was a shady character. Something didn't feel right about him, and I also had a feeling that he took no responsibility for anything, He refused to come forward, but wanted Holly to know that he was there. I could not get a full view of his face. Whenever I tried to see him, he would shake his head no, and stay hidden. This confirmed what I was feeling about this man.

I told Holly, "Grandma holds a bird in her hand. She was very loving to you. She gave you unconditional love. She gave conditional love to your father. They did not get along in life, but do get along there. He is with her and she supports him. When she was alive, she made pies, canned, and did a lot of cooking. She especially enjoyed making berry pies. I see many knick-knacks scattered through her house."

Holly validated so many of the things I had revealed in this reading. She told me that her grandma had three main men in her life. She kicked her first husband out of the house because he was a drunk. His oldest son changed his last name to his mother's maiden name in order to not be responsible for his father's debts. She did not marry the next man she was involved with, because he was still married to another woman whom he had left. He died when Holly's father was about four or five years old. She married the next man and remained with him until she crossed over. He was a little pudgy in the stomach and had thinning hair. Holly had a picture of her grandma standing in a dress with a high, white collar, very much like the one I described. Holly told me that she wore aprons that tied around the back and tied shoes. She also wore rolled hose. Grandma always had a bird that was a canary or parakeet—and she was noted for all the knick-knacks she had throughout her house. In fact, she had over a hundred pair of salt and pepper shakers. She cooked a lot and canned and the client remembers the berry pies.

The intention in sharing their readings with you is to let you know that spirit comes through and displays their life for you so that you can recognize their presence. They are not usually embarrassed by sharing their life's stories but would rather display to you that they are there and care about your life. Even through death, their connection to you is as important for you as it is for them.

PART IV
Higher Education

the STUDENT'S PERSPECTIVE

"A vision is the ability to see what some only dream.
To act on a vision is like reaching for the moon,
knowing the stars are there to catch you!"

It was January, 2004, and I was returning to Peace River with Christine and April. Sandy had set up a class that she was calling P7. It was the class for certification as a teacher. Sandy and John Maerz had decided to develop a program that would qualify students to teach the "Anastasi System of Psychic Development" and this was a first step for them. Though the program was still in its developmental stages, Sandy and John Maerz said that, in order to be certified, I would have to retake six months of her seminars as an observer or student teacher, and then I would be required to teach a series of classes with her. After this, I'd be a certified "Anastasi System" teacher!

Sandy and John wanted to expand the teaching of their curriculum by having others teach it. Sandy was a good teacher and had a curriculum that delivered some great results. However, I knew that my own teaching would include the valuable experiences of learning from Mic, Patti, and other motivational speakers. At the time I didn't think I'd ever be able to just teach the Anastasi method.

Working with Sandy to get certified to teach her classes would also be a financial challenge. It would require me to return to Florida monthly for the next seven months. And I'd have to make arrangements to student-teach a class with her. All of this would certainly require some leaps of faith.

At this point, the plan was to set up a class in Minneapolis by the fall of 2003. By now, I had shared with Sandy and John my desire to teach and do readings nationwide. They even thought that I might be interested in working with students who were pursuing their student teaching certification.

I was excited about being able to travel, do readings, teach Sandy's system and expand what I saw as possibilities. However, Christine was a little more reserved where Sandy and John were concerned. We both wanted to grow and develop Introspect...A Look Within and at the same time help Sandy. Sandy had become a friend and mentor. Knowing that they were struggling financially, I felt that if we were to grow, they should, too. I also knew that Sandy wanted to teach and work outside of Starchild's facility more. She said she liked the idea of more freedom and independence. If I could help Sandy realize this, I wanted to do what I could.

Christine warned me that even though the intentions were pure, John Maerz and I did not like each other. She thought that problems might arise when Sandy was away teaching with us. She also reminded me that they were only developing this plan, and felt that they had a tendency to view me as a perpetual student on whom to test their marketing plans, rather than as a colleague.

Christie and I checked into the Holiday Inn's room 130, as we have done so many times in the past, and I cherished the thought of being here for the next months. I could take in this view and enjoy the feelings I had about this journey a little longer. I knew that someday I would miss this spot, but I already carried it with me every day. I used this vision of the bridges over the river every day. That evening at Peace River was like coming home.

Early the next morning, at 4 a.m., Friar's wake-up call went off. I stayed in bed for a few moments just relaxing. It wasn't long until I wanted to get up to look out at the bridges that span Peace River. The lights that lined the bridges still twinkled in the river below. I was so happy to be back to this area. The hotel had reserved room 130 for nearly all of my visits to Peace River and it really did feel like a home away from home.

Out on the grass I could see a vision of my dad and me. I was about six years old, standing on his toes as he waltzed me around to the song, "Tennessee Waltz." I could see my grandmother laughing and clapping as my dad danced with me.

I could see Wayne and Friar smiling as I enjoyed the rising of the sun. I was waiting for the moment when I could go out and feed the seagulls.

I had spent countless hours out by the water, feeding the seagulls and taking in that calm of the bay at Peace River. I found myself thinking back to the previous night and the trip I made to a local service station and convenience store to buy the eight loaves of bread. The person behind the counter looked at my purchase of eight loaves of bread and asked, "What are you going to do with all that bread?" I responded,

"I am taking them over to the hotel to feed the seagulls." She quickly stated, "I don't know why you would want to feed them; they are so selfish." Without hesitation, I looked at this woman and replied, "Do you mean they are like some humans?" I envisioned the seagulls eating, noticing that some come close to be fed, while other stay back and fight over what is there. And, then I looked up into her eyes and said, "We all deserve to eat and be cared about." She was silent. It was at that moment that I realized how much of an influence Friar's guidance had on me and how seriously I felt about what I was learning.

After taking my shower and getting ready for the day, I went out to feed the seagulls. Standing outside feeding the seagulls was relaxing, and for the first time pelicans joined in the morning feasting activities. They were new, and it took me by surprise; there were two of them. The seagulls came by the dozens and it didn't take long to go through the eight loaves of bread.

I noticed that my guides were gathering on the dock. I saw Wayne and Friar with some of the other guides that I had seen from time to time. Indian Chief, the Mohawk brave, the Tibetan monk, the tall white-haired gentleman with pale blue eyes that helped me to write, and the woman with the white dress and dove on her shoulder were all conversing together. I couldn't hear them, but I could see them. It was as if they were having a casual meeting of some kind. I didn't know at this time how many guides worked with me, but I did know that when I went exploring for this information, they were not ready to tell me. I had learned that the Greek gentleman, the Mohawk brave and Indian Chief, were part of my protection. The Tibetan monk wouldn't break silence and talk to me; he just prayed a lot. I wondered what he would say when he chose to speak. The lady in the white dress seemed to be angelic and she always had doves around her, but I didn't know her purpose. And, of course there was Friar. He and I had already built such a strong relationship. He was and still is the one in charge and who filters information for me as I work. Friar is the one that I rely on the most. My brother, Wayne, had always been right there with Friar, but I didn't know if he would continue to stay or if he was there for just awhile. It didn't matter; I enjoyed my brother's presence and will always be grateful for his help and for his believing in me, even when I didn't.

I had the feeling that this weekend was going to be interesting because I had never seen them gather like this and I really wondered what this meant. But no one was sharing! It made me feel a little uneasy.

I headed back to the hotel room and Christie, April, and I locked up the room and went to breakfast before heading to Starchild. Everyone was unusually quite. I figured it was because we didn't know what to expect that day. All that Sandy had told us was that it would be challenging. She shared with us that we would be discussing the dynamic of teaching psychic development. That was all we knew.

Christine and April attended this mandatory class with the idea that they probably wouldn't go any further, at least not at this time. They would wait until I was teaching and perhaps then go through certification to save the travel expenses. Sandy had discussed the fact that I would be able to teach with student teachers once I was certified. We were setting the goal of completing the psychic teaching certification during the summer of 2003. Sandy agreed to come and teach with me until she felt I was ready to do it on my own. It turns out that I received my teacher's certificate on July 27, 2003. I was the first Starchild student to achieve that goal.

When we arrived at Starchild that morning in 2003, we were surprised to see only four of us in attendance. Sandy, John, and Ed were teaching this class. Ed began teaching during our mediumship classes, after Jason had left. Ed was a very quiet person and was noted for doing a session called "Messages" once a month on a Saturday evening. We were planning on attending it that night.

We had a great time during the discussions about what we could expect for a curriculum. Sandy, John, and Ed taught a session on keeping a class in order and what, as teachers, we might expect dealing with during a class.

Each of us had to teach a segment of the class curriculum to the other students and in front of the teachers. We could pick the part we wanted to do. Christie chose to teach pendulum use and I chose psychometry.

In this segment, Sandy's intention was to demonstrate how students can take control of your class. She wanted us to learn how this kind of disruption can throw the class schedule off. The teachers and the students in the class were expected to come up with reasons to break the pace. I watched the first student get up and teach her segment. One student took a bathroom break in the middle of everything, then someone from the store came in for a phone call, and the disruptions went on and on. As we did this, the student teachers were expected to continue teaching, keeping as many students engaged as possible despite the interruptions, and to stay focused, and on target.

Christie's turn came and several people bombarded her with interruptions. Some had to leave the room and other asked questions that veered off from the material she was presenting, but she was doing well. I excused myself to leave several times. With others coughing and carrying on, Christie lost it and decided to hold the classroom's door shut so that I couldn't return to the room. As she was holding one door shut, I went out of the store and came around through the rear door of the room. I stuck my head in through the back door and said, "Boo!" Christie, who was still holding the other door shut, fell to the ground laughing. In fact, the whole class lost it; every one was laughing, teachers included. I guess the class they were teaching was officially out of control.

At the close of the day we had decided to go to the "Messages" session with Ed. There were about eighteen people in attendance. When Ed gave me a reading, he said he saw a guide, the Mohawk brave, riding on his horse, and he was running into a tarot card. I later looked up the tarot card that he said was in the Rider Deck. The card represented challenge. I think my guide was giving me a warning of what was coming the next day.

We met Mic after class for a healing session for each of us. It was already 10 p.m., but we were determined to get the healings that night. I had sessions with Mic almost every time that I visited Florida. This four day stay was no exception.

The healing sessions that week would focus on identifying what resonated for me in what I was learning, and on clearing and strengthening my auric, or energy field so that I could build additional protection around myself. Building a stronger protection around myself was an essential part of my development. My intention was to continue to work with mediumship and add teaching as part of my mission. It was important for me to take care of my physical, emotional, and spiritual well being so that I could help more people.

The next morning, when we arrived at class, the teachers announced that we were going to do what they referred to as a "Psychic Shakedown." The purpose of this session was to teach us to recognize the different ways that people, knowingly or unknowingly, can psychically invade you.

They were going to teach us how to handle the kind of interference that can happen during readings and teaching by having us feel the psychic pushes that such interference creates. All of us felt nervous that we were going to be asked to stand up in front of the teachers and do readings for as long as we could. They were going to bombard us with whatever psychic stuff they could, and we were to continue for as long as we could using protections and techniques that we had learned in class. Relying on these techniques as well as our natural abilities, we were expected to continue to do spirit communication through any challenge they presented until we chose to stop.

My session continued for almost two hours before I chose to stop. Throughout, I felt the streams of energy they passed my way in order to interfere with the reading. I read the woman named Anna Lisa, and brought in a friend of hers who had passed away. The deceased woman showed herself sitting by a desk, and pushed the wheeled desk chair across the floor. Apparently the woman had been confined to a wheel chair. As the reading continued, I could feel the invasions that John and Sandy where pushing at me, trying to give me the jitters. I recognized that this excited energy was not mine and pushed it off me. They sent many different kinds of emotions to me, but I didn't even feel many of them and the ones I did, I acknowledged and dismissed. But John and Sandy still continued in other ways to get through to me.

Then I started a second reading for John and brought his grandfather through. I described his house on the east coast and his grandfather's garage out back of the house, and all the gardening he did. I could see the attacks they were attempting to make and Ed even pushed a red tractor telepathically into my reading, but I recognized it didn't fit.

Toward the end of my session, Sandy was out the door and attacking me through the wall. I could feel it and did protective shielding to stop the attacks, but she continued until finally I felt tagged in my heart chakra and stopped the reading. John said that I could continue if I chose and I said, "No, I choose to not continue!"

Each of us withstood the test, but it felt like a very long day. After the session, Sandy said she was going to give me a psychic slap, which is similar to a physical slap, and she said that it would probably give me a headache. She wasn't able to succeed, though. I had been working very extensively with Mic on protecting myself, and all of my work obviously paid off!

This session helped April realize that she does way too much reading by using telepathy or her third eye. As a very strong-minded person, and having already taken the series of classes with Sandy and John, she was disappointed that they had not shared this with her earlier. We made a pact that we would work together to get her through this issue. She found out that doing mediumship through telepathy caused physical problems, because the energy would get trapped in her head. It was important that she learn to be a clear channel and let the energy flow through her. She has since accomplished the correct techniques.

At the close of the day, we felt ready to go back to the hotel, take hot baths, and order room service. We were all tired. The weekend opened the door to a new phase in my life; sitting in on the classes at Starchild, and beginning to student-teach.

From February until June, I went to Florida several times a month, completing the requirements that Sandy and John had decided upon. They hadn't had anybody do this before, and they were busy working out the kinks as they arose.

When I first agreed to do this, we decided that I would go through one series of student teaching and observation. Toward the end of the series, they decided it would have be two, which technically would have doubled my time in Florida. We agreed that I could watch two different series of classes at one time to keep on track. They had two different groups of students going through the curriculum. One group was working on mediumship, and the other was in the first part of the psychic development series.

Sandy and I had long talks about the future. I shared with her that I wanted to start teaching soon, and she said that she felt I was ready to do that. In fact, we made plans that she would come up and teach in Minnesota. I also let her know that, although I would teach her curriculum, I felt it wasn't complete without bringing in the other things I had learned while in Florida. I was referring to what I learned from Mic and Patti. She said she didn't have an issue with that, as long as I taught everything she taught, too.

By now, I was licensed in Florida to do readings. I was busy gaining experience with every opportunity that opened up to me. I was doing group and individual readings, and working on teaching.

At home, we were busy working, too.

the EVENTS

"When something is difficult and people are challenged,
the challenge can make us one or one alone.
The true challenge is choice!"

Things were moving along fairly well, but they certainly weren't profitable at this point. In fact, Christie and my venture was running in the red financially and we knew it would be awhile before that turned around.

Mic was coming up to Minneapolis fairly regularly, as was April. We were doing private as well as gallery readings, and Mic was offering healing sessions. We were on the radio and, when Mic was in town, we brought him on as well.

We even rented a booth at the Mind Body Life Expo. It was a great experience for all of us. Mic, April, Christie, and I were working and handing out information about Introspect…A Look Within, and what we were all about.

We broke even with some of the events and on others we ended up in the red. We were told by our guides to hang in there, and that it would eventually change as we became better known.

Even with the money issues, we decided to take a leap of faith and develop a program that we could put on at different venues and perhaps even take on the road, if we chose.

We had planned to stage our first attempt at a small venue, but the smaller theaters in our area were not available when we wanted them. So we decided to use an auditorium, with the idea that we would work on filling the first floor only and would leave the balcony in reserve. We chose the historic Northrup Auditorium on the University of Minnesota campus, which has a capacity of about 1500.

Sandy, Mic, and Patti, along with some other teachers and some fellow graduates, all agreed to participate. Sandy wanted John Maerz and Ed Hicks to be included. The budget was so tight, and as we were committing money to advertising, we didn't have a lot left over.

We provided Sandy, John Maerz, and Mic with a salary commitment and an agreement to pay their hotel and airfare charges. With this, we were assured that the principle people would be there.

Christine and I decided that we would surprise Sandy. We felt that her students should reward her for her years of dedication to the field. By then, we had started teaching Sandy's system in Minnesota, and we thought it would be great if John Edward would be willing to come and surprise her. We knew she was very proud of him and his work. We decided to send an e-mail to John Edward to see if he would be interested in joining us to thank Sandy for all her hard work. At the time I read his book, he had mentioned something about her being the only person who could claim to be his teacher, and I knew he was having her on his television show to talk about her work. Asking him seemed like the natural thing to do, and what a surprise for Sandy if he accepted!

We prepared for the show; it would offer readings, a salute to Sandy and John Edward, if he came, and we were designing the show to encompass the classes and more.

After several weeks, we were notified by e-mail that John Edward declined the invitation due to previous commitments. We had decided, prior to receiving his response, that we would continue with the show either way. Former students were planning to come, and we thought we would still be able to do it.

We advertised on television, radio, and in print. We went on air to do readings and to advertise the upcoming show.

The ticket price started at $25.00 and went up from there, depending on the seat location. We soon realized that tickets were not selling well, and we were a bit apprehensive about continuing. In the end, the ticket sales were not anywhere near where we hoped, but the people attending the show felt that they got a great experience.

Following the show, we staged a psychic fair at the Airport Hilton Hotel. It brought in work for the people who flew into Minneapolis, and gave the public an opportunity to have a private reading with Sandy or any of us who were involved with the show.

The show brought challenges for all of us. For the audience, it offered a glimpse of how much more there is than what we physically see.

The pressure of creating, developing, and producing the show strained my relationship with Christine. There had been long hours of work, arranging the advertising and the venue layout, gathering the extra money that was needed for unexpected expenses, and attending to other things that needed completion. In the end, the challenges strengthened our relationship and we learned how important it is to stay in sync with each other as we move forward. It was this event that taught Christie and I to notice the weak links in planning and resolve them early on. This experience gave us information that we will be able to use for years to come.

Some others did not fare as well as Christie and me. Patti and Mic, upon returning to Florida, decided to go their separate ways. Mic moved out of their home, and Patti eventually created a new home for herself.

Classmates were at their best, offering to help at every and any turn. It was a learning experience for everyone.

Personally, the experience validated that I was capable, and could do my psychic work on a stage. It was challenging to walk out on a stage and discover that you could not see the faces of the audience members because of the lighting. What surprised me was that, even under the lighting restrictions, Christine and I were able to pick up the streams of energy and go to the person that the reading was for and complete the reading. The work does still happen, even under adverse conditions!

For example, during the show I went to the left side of the auditorium and put my hand out and said I had a man who was coming through, saying he died in a car accident. I said I felt like he is brother to someone in front of me, and that he left behind two children and a wife. No one spoke up. I continued the reading and said that the woman whose reading this was, was sitting straight back from where I was standing. I stood in front of the row and pointed, moving my arm in a straight line. I said "Right back there; the woman who came with her friend." A woman in the area to which I was pointing stood up, but said she didn't recognize the man as her brother.

This was very frustrating, because her brother was insistent and we were about to break at the mid-point of the show. I realized that this woman must have felt like she had amnesia about a relative, or that she felt like a deer in front of headlights, frozen. I gave her more information and she just stood there shocked. I kidded around and said, "Well, if you don't want to acknowledge him, does anyone want to adopt him?" We then took a break in the show.

During the break, the woman approached the stage and asked for me. I came out and she apologized, saying that she had drawn a blank earlier. She said that it was her brother, and that the description of him and how he died fit exactly. After break, I started the remainder of the show by joking, "Her brother got adopted! She recognized him while we were on break."

Christine had also done a reading for someone on the left side of the stage. As she gave detailed information, the person was not coming forward. I stepped up next to Christine and said, "This information is for Mary; she is right there." I drew a line directly to her. She stood up, and acknowledged the reading was hers and validated the information.

The most notable reading that I remember of the show involved a father who was determined to come through. I pointed back to one side of the auditorium and pointed down the row to where a woman was sitting. I said "This reading is for you. There are three generations of breast cancer in your family, and your father sees the fight you are having. He is giving you thumbs up; you will win. He wants you to know that at Christmas (this was November) your Christmas lights are going to give you a bit of trouble." "Take heart," I continued, "it is your Dad getting through to let you know he is with you." The woman later called and validated the information, and asked that if he had anything else to share, would I please let her know.

When I watched the tape of the show, I realized once again how much these messages mean to people and why I am doing this work.

I had been terrified to go on that stage that day, but when my feet hit the wood, the fears were replaced with the joy of being in the moment, with guidance all around, and doing what made my heart sing!

Would we do it again? Yes! With the right support and timing, we'd do it in a heartbeat! We gained some new students, and everyone went away with more than they had anticipated. It wasn't an easy one, but it was a good day!

To date, the reading that has had the most meaning for me was what I had witnessed in New Orleans. Christine and I decided to do a two year anniversary trip to New Orleans. John Edward was doing his show, as he had done one year prior, and we contacted April to see if she wanted to join us there to read for two or three days in honor of the journey. She gave a definite yes!

We intended to go there and read as many people as possible. We wanted to give an opportunity to those interested in hearing from a loved one on the other side. As Christie and I reviewed our plans, we wondered if John Edward would be interested in what we were doing. For us, it was about the work, connecting two worlds to bring closure or healing to the person who has passed and the person who is here.

We thought it would be great if John took an interest in helping us promote what we were planning. Perhaps he could increase the number of mediums available to do the readings. We felt it would be an opportunity for some of those 1500 guests to get a reading they wanted so badly, but whose odds of receiving one from John Edward were so low.

I e-mailed John's office to let them know what we were planning and ask if they had any interest in helping us, but this time I received no response.

I shared with Christine that two years prior was the turning point for me and it was the reason I was now working in this field. I do feel what we do betters people's lives. It helps people realize that there is more than what we see physically. Each reading is a testimonial; we are loved and cared about even in the face of death and the loss of people we love. It validates for each of us that our love is still returned, and in this, it is as if heaven's gates are wide open and we are allowed to touch and be touched with God's infinite grace.

We thought the timing was perfect. We rented a room for the readings at the hotel we had stayed at previously; the Hilton Garden at Lake Pontchatrain in New Orleans.

We set a fee for the readings that was less than what we would normally charge. The object was to read as many people as time allowed and charge what we thought we needed to in order to cover our expenses. This trip had such personal meaning for me that I would have done it for free if I could have afforded it.

The three of us did readings for two long days. We worked from 10 a.m. until well after midnight. We took only short breaks for lunch and dinner.

We had made arrangements to close during Mr. Edward's show so that we could see him work, as we had the previous year. To my amazement, he did not use the birthday party analogy. I have always been impressed with John and his work and was happy to see him lose the birthday party reference. For those not receiving a reading, it didn't feel anything like a birthday party!

As I sat through the show and observed the people there, I was reminded once again of why I chose to make such a change in my life. John's work and the audience gave validation to the importance of my own journey and why I wished to continue on it.

We left just before the show was over so that we could set up and return to work. We returned to work about 9 p.m., and planned on reading until 11 p.m. that night. At midnight, I walked out into the hall and saw a line of people still there. Looking at the appointment book and then looking back at the people who were still waiting, I said, "Okay, who here doesn't belong? The appointments are full and there are more people here than we have appointments for!" A lady quickly quipped back, "Hey, you are psychic; you should know!" I looked at her and asked, "Are you on the schedule?" She said, "Yes." I replied, "Well, I may be psychic but you are paying for a reading. What does that say?" Everyone laughed and it lightened things up in the late hours of the night, as people were sitting around waiting for their private reading. We had been reading for approximately ten hours.

The lady with her daughter walked up to me and said, "I don't have an appointment, but I have been sitting here all evening and was hoping you'd see me before you leave. I went to John's show and I didn't get a reading."

She started to cry. I asked her to just wait a minute. I went in and asked Christine and April if either wanted to take one more reading. Both said no because they were very tired. I returned to the hall with the news but, as I looked up at her, she reminded me that this was the very reason I came. I showed her to my table and I gave her a reading.

During the reading, her sister came in and showed me that she had fallen from a balcony. It was no accident and the death had been investigated, but the police couldn't prove anything. I continued to share with her the information her deceased sister was giving me. Her sister on the other side stated that she had gotten herself into trouble, owing money to ruthless people. She said that she took responsibility for the circumstances surrounding her death. Her deceased sister then told me that the woman sitting before me was having a lot of financial issues and that I should tell her, "Don't feel you let me down." In fact, the sister from the other side stated that the woman needed to let go of the commitment she felt she owed her sister. The sister on the other side said, "My sister owes nothing!"

At the end of reading, the woman confirmed that her ex-husband had spent an inheritance they had and that she has very little money. She was carrying a lot of guilt because, due to a lack of money, she hasn't been able to afford a stone for her sister's grave!

She showed me a card that she had taken to Mr. Edward's show. The card was written by her sister before she passed, and in it her sister stated how much she loved her and how thankful she was to have her in her life. I asked her if she believed what her deceased sister wrote, and if she ever considered what she would have written to her sister in return. It would make sense that they had only gratitude for the time they shared together in this life and for the love they shared. The validation of her sister's love and forgiveness were present already in that card!

When the reading finally ended and the woman wanted to pay me, I looked at her and said, "You owe me nothing. You validated for me why I do this work and you did it on the anniversary of some major decisions I made in my life." I thanked her for coming! The woman hugged me and tearfully thanked me for the reading.

This reading was a very heartfelt experience for me, and now I'd like to share with you a special moment in my personal life.

It was February, 2004, and my husband, Jeff, and I had decided to go to Hawaii to see famous psychics and authors Sylvia Browne and John Edward do their work. I had never seen Sylvia Browne before. We decided we would spend a week on Waikiki Beach together. It had been a long time since we had had a vacation together and we both were looking forward to this time.

We stayed at the Marriott, which faced Waikiki Beach. The first morning there, when we were getting ready for the day, we both looked at each other and asked, "What would you like to do?" We had been so busy working that it seemed strange to get up and not know what was scheduled. I suggested we go over to the beach and people watch, just hang out. As we were heading there, I mentioned that my dad and mom had been there and that my dad always talked about going back there. He died before he had a chance.

I mentioned that one of my favorite movies growing up was *Gidget Goes Hawaiian*. I think some of the stars were Deborah Walley and James Darren. I was in my early teens when I first saw it and thought it was a fun movie. At that age, I liked the teeny bopper, boy-gets-girl-girl-gets-boy movies. I told Jeff that I thought the guy they called "Eddie" in the movie performed at the Almoana Hotel. I asked Jeff if he knew where that was or if it really existed. He replied that he had no idea.

We walked across the street and something in the sky caught my husband's eye. Before long, both of us were starring at it. It looked like two balloons tied together. It seemed out of place. All of a sudden, a gentleman walked up to us. He was wearing swimming trunks that revealed a thick waist and his hairline reminded me of my dad's. The gentlemen asked, "Hey kids, what are you looking at?"

At the time, I was fifty-four years old. This gentleman was probably in his late seventies or early eighties. I replied that I had no idea, but pointed to what we were looking at. The gentleman walked away only to return shortly after. He handed my husband a pair of binoculars and I noticed Friar looking kind of funny standing on the beach in his brown robe. He lifted his robe to show his feet, and he was wearing lime colored plastic sandals. I just smiled thinking that Friar's sense of humor always surprised me and caught me off guard. He said to me, "Why don't you extend your hand?" I reached out my hand and said, "Hi, I am Susan and this is my husband Jeff." The gentleman replied that his name was Keith. He then asked, "Where are you kids from?" I replied, "Minneapolis, Minnesota." He smiled and said, "I have a daughter who lives there!" "Okay," I thought, "what a coincidence!" I asked him where he was from and his reply was, "I am from Argyle, Minnesota." Now, I have never met anyone from Argyle in all of my life, but it was my dad's home town. This was one of those "a-ha" moments. He asked where we were staying and I told him, and then I asked him where he was staying. He replied, "Almoana Hotel." What a great way to start our vacation! He said he fell in love with the place and he comes here for three months every year.

As we walked away, my husband said, "There are so many coincidences in what just happen that it would have been easier to win the lottery!" It was a wonderful experience and it set the tone for the week.

TIME OUT

"Transition takes us off autopilot.
Intention puts you in the pilot's seat."

Sandy and her partner John kept referring to me as their first child. They were still developing their system for teachers and I was not privy to their detailed plans.

The heartache started when I had an opportunity to teach a seminar in Sarasota. By then, Sandy and John had opened up teaching certification to others and I had been doing readings in the area and had developed a clientele through Patti Star.

I shared with Sandy that I had the opportunity to open up a class in Sarasota, about ninety miles away from Starchild. I also let her know that, in my experience, no one there had heard of her or her business. I thought it would be neat to bring her up there and do the classes along with her and Christine. Since my intention was to work there only periodically, I thought it would be nice to get their name out in that area.

She said it sounded good and that we'd go together.

To date, Introspect had been paying the expenses for the classes we were holding in Minneapolis, including Sandy's and John's airfare and hotel rooms when they came. They received a fee for materials and a share of the profits, if there were any. We were willing to work the same way in Sarasota. The burden of the expenses was on my shoulders.

I had been working in Sarasota and staying at Peace River. My phone rang and it was Sandy asking me to meet her and John at a restaurant for breakfast. She wanted to talk to me before I left for home.

The previous day, I'd had a healing with Mic and he said that I would be working through issues pertaining to my mother and dad's relationship. I couldn't understand what he was referring to and perhaps. I thought, it was his mom and dad's relationship he was focusing in on. I thought it was strange that it would come up, because I didn't have an issue with dad and mom and their relationship. It was always kept very separate from us children and I didn't carry any baggage about it. I had been hoping to meet Mic that morning if I had time; I was supposed to call him.

I arrived at the diner for breakfast just as Sandy and John walked in. John seemed upset, and he commented that setting up shop so close to my mentors' store was no way to honor them.

As John explained his point of view, I tuned into the guidance that was all around us. Friar was holding his hands out as if to comfort me, and I heard him say, "It isn't wise to say too much; just listen! All will be shown soon." The Tibetan monk was praying and the Indian Chief stood directly behind John with his arms crossed, as he listened to all the words that John wasn't saying.

The Chief said, "He is already planning to have people work the area and they are territorializing the teaching!"

That day, my guides showed me that Sandy and John were keeping things from me. For my part, I had the excitement of a child able to do something special for people she cared about. I thought I could help them expand their business north and we would be able to work together to realize this vision. I trusted and believed in these two people and Sandy felt like family. I felt I was honoring what they taught me by growing and developing, while always representing them in a positive light by increasing awareness of their work and dedication. I was so surprised by what John was saying and by what Sandy wasn't saying that I felt as if I were out of body.

John accused me of always trying to stretch the rules as we went, but how could I be doing that when the rules themselves were being set as we went along? In fact, I never really knew the rules.

I felt very hurt and disillusioned. I had the best intentions and was being told something different. I asked if we could teach the class at the store which would mean the clients would have to travel an hour and a half each way for two days a month and he said, "No." Their classes weren't full and unless they were, it would not be an option. I remember thinking, "That is odd; I was told that they were starting to fill up." I looked up at Friar and he stood with his hands outstretched and reassured me that it would be revealed later.

Driving up to Sarasota later that morning, I forgot to call Mic and let him know that I couldn't meet with him. I needed to get to the airport so I wouldn't miss my plane.

But I did think, "Mic was right. He wasn't referring to my mom and dad but to Sandy and John."

Friar was right. Their plans couldn't include me because they wanted to build a territorial psychic network. I didn't want to be part of it because I felt that it allowed for only limited self-empowerment and growth. I believe in empowering people to strive and grow. This has always been my intention in teaching!

On the plane trip home, I thought about my visit to Florida, and that I had spent a couple of days at the beginning of the trip staying with Patti in Sarasota before going to Peace River.

In particular, I thought about an hour or two we had spent at a house belonging to one of her friends. Bill had called and asked Patti if she could stop over, as he was having some issues with his back. When we arrived at Bill's house, he was playing a taped interview with Joseph Campbell. My attention was drawn to the television since I was familiar with some of his ideas. On my wall at home, I have a quotation by this gentleman. He says something like, "We must be willing to let go of the life we planned, so as to have the life that is awaiting us." In the interview Bill was playing, Mr. Campbell was talking about rites of passage and how they can be very painful. As I remembered this scene, I felt tears well up as I saw Friar bowing his head to me. At that moment, I knew that the journey was about to change and that I would grow in a different direction.

RITE *of* PASSAGE

"Little lotus, you honor the flower
by unfolding in all your beauty."

Our classes reflected all of the Florida experiences as well as
a lifetime of lessons. And over and over, the students remarked
how the classes had changed their lives. They were all doing
so much better in their lives.

During the time after I separated from John Maerz and
Sandy, new avenues opened for Introspect…A Look Within.
And although my preference would have been to continue
to work with Sandy, I later realized it was indeed time to
grow and move forward. Sometimes the help you need to
push the door open so you do not become complacent
comes from unexpected sources, and I guess it was my turn
to get pushed.

Christie and I took some time off from teaching our
classes to seriously consider what we wanted to do. I was

planning on returning to Florida to do healing work with my friends for awhile. I thought that I would take some time to spend with my family and do some private readings. What I really needed was time to regroup and heal.

During a month stay in Long Island, Christie and I decided that, even though I had certification from Starchild, I didn't need to continue on that path. It was time to step out of the mentors' shadows and start our own journey. With the encouragement and support of past and present students, we developed our own classes, *Inner Journey*© and *Bridging Two Worlds.*© They are written from our experiences in extra-sensory development, and the self-motivational and develop-mental techniques that we have learned. They also resonate with reiki and t'ai chi, as well as shamanic, aromatherapeu-thic, oriental and other healing arts. We feel that it isn't enough to just teach psychic development. We have devel-oped a safe and protective environment, where our students are taught respectfully to discover what resonates for them. We offer many perspectives because it is important to teach the whole person to be whole.

We feel our classes are a tribute to the journey and to our mentors who, for a time, came in to help guide us.

We now share with our students what the "rite of passage" is, and we let them know that wherever they go, and whatever they do, we wish them the best. And the truest way to honor your mentors is to fulfill your capabilities. One of our students remarked that he had heard a quotation that went something like this: "A disciple does his master a great injus-tice if he remains a disciple." We do not want our students to remain our students, but to strive to be all they can be and to always grow and learn. It is all about evolution.

PART V
Life Goes On

PSYCHIC 411

"In the solitude, a light breaks
through the clouds to shine and light your path.
The light is called guidance."

The hardest information for any psychic to receive is information about him or herself, or someone the psychic is close to. It requires the psychic to get out of his or her own way. Often our own desires get in the way of our ability to discern the truth. When we teach our classes, we refer to the doctor who is better off getting an objective opinion from another doctor than he is treating himself. If you channel or are connecting with your Higher Self, you have access to all the information, but our minds can interject what we wish to know when we are too close to the subject.

In class, we do teach methods to help students receive information about their own situations, but we also suggest they get a second opinion from someone that is very good! It is just like going to a specialist in the field when you need that second opinion.

There are several people who are accessible, excellent in their fields, and who I trust to give me accurate information about myself. After my rite of passage and all the things that had been happening, Christie suggested that we get two readings from people who use different styles, and then compare the information we received.

Her first suggestion, was since we were already planning to travel to New York, that I look up Glenn Dove. I had a reading by Glenn a year before and enjoyed his spirit communication skills immensely. Glenn lives in Long Island and has an office in Baldwin. I remember the first time I met him. He walked into the reception area of his office and I was greeted by a tall, good-looking gentleman who introduced himself as Glenn. I usually can tell in the first five seconds if I am going to like somebody, and he seemed very sweet.

As I sat with him through the reading, I noticed that he drew on a piece of paper with a pen to help him concentrate as he did his reading. I hadn't seen that before. During the reading, Glenn brought in my father, Glenn. It surprised him to see that they shared a name. Glenn brought in about six or seven relatives and, because he didn't know me very well, he learned quickly that not all the spirits in the room belonged there. Many belonged to upcoming clients. He spent time distinguishing my relatives from the others so that he could do my reading. The first reading was all about the book I was working on, which is this book. He picked up on it right away, because my dad came carrying it to him. Glenn was very good! There was something about him that I couldn't place, but I knew I would learn about it when the time was right.

I called and set up an appointment with him for Christie and another for me. I was wondering what the spirits would have to say this time.

I was excited that my daughter was going to meet him on this trip. On the day of our appointments, Christie had her reading first, and then it was my turn. In my reading, Glenn received information about the classes we were developing and talked about how he saw the materials delivered to the students. It was really a nice validation of the work we were doing on *Inner Journey*© and *Bridging Two Worlds*© courses, and he was seeing them all complete! He talked about my experiences over the past months and said that it was a way of cleaning house. He said that I needed to be clear of some of these ties so that I'd be free to develop what was coming. He stated that the fall and winter seasons would be very busy, and that 2005 would be even busier. He suggested that I take time to rest now, because there wouldn't be as much time very soon.

He shared with me his interest in teaching, and we got together later to discuss his interests and what teaching options he might be interested in. This was what I couldn't place that last time I had seen him. We enjoyed our readings that day, and still enjoy keeping in touch with him.

We scheduled our second readings with Lydia Clar about a month later. Lydia is located in Florida and available for psychic readings over the phone. She is one of the best psychics in her field and is mentioned throughout John Edward's work. She was the noted psychic who told him when he was young that someday he would be doing what he now does. She is open about sharing with her clients all that she receives during the reading. This would be my first reading with Lydia. She was the psychic that Christie suggested I call when Wayne passed away, but at that time, I was drawn to Sandy.

When I spoke with Lydia during our phone appointment, she shared her insights about what she saw coming. It was Lydia who validated for me what the students had already been expressing, namely that the work we were doing had improved their lives and was important to them. Lydia did not know my connection with Sandy but she knew to be gentle with me when she said that mentors had come into my life to help me. "But," she continued, "you have outgrown them and you are no longer a student whether they feel you are or you feel you are."

Lydia helped me realize that it was now time for new experiences and growth. I felt like a bird just kicked out of the warm nest. Lydia stated that she saw the next months as a period of reflection and writing. After that, the fall and winter, she said, would be extremely busy. She felt what I was doing would expand and grow in the new year, 2005. I remember thinking, "I can handle that."

I felt very good that these two different psychics gave me basically the same information. I had told Christine I didn't know who I could trust, and her suggestions gave validations for me. I felt I got the validations and direction I needed to proceed with my vision. I had felt very insecure about my path after experiencing my rite of passage, and now a door was opened that helped me see more objectively where I was at and where I needed to be.

I felt like a huge weight had lifted off of me and I had desire to continue the journey.

GOOD MORNING CLASS

*"In the twilight hours of the morning, I reach my hand out
and I am touched by an angel sent from the heavens.
And a gift is delivered; we call it a new day."*

The three most common questions that students ask when
inquiring about classes are: 1) Could I be psychic? 2) Did you
always know you were psychic? and 3) How long will it take
for me to develop my skills?

The first question is my favorite. Each student that I have
taught and each client that I've read, without exception,
brings something to me that reminds me of myself. It is like
seeing my reflection in a lake.

Once, a woman came for a reading, accompanied by her
husband and another couple. They were going to get readings
and healings that night with some of the psychics and healers
who were in town for the Mind Body Life Expo that we were

participating in. I recalled the conversation I had with her when she booked the reading. She had been to an event previously and a psychic told her that she had a third eye. She asked me if this was true, and wanted to know what she could do with it if it was true. I told her that I would explain everything when we met.

After she came and the reading was over, I answered her question. I shared with her that the third eye is the sixth chakra or energy center that is located between the eyebrows. I explained that it is thought by most to be indigo in color and is associated with telepathy and clairvoyance. I explained that in spiritual teachings it is the center of "I see," or intuition or psychic ability.

This woman's questions reminded me of the innocence of children when they first discover that boys and girls are different. She was genuinely excited about the discovery and the possibility that she might be psychic.

I continued to explain that I believed we are all psychic, and that being psychic is a part of each of us. Some have learned to ignore it for so long that they don't remember the abilities that accompanied them at birth. Have you ever seen a newborn baby? It looks all around, though doctors say that newborn infants don't see very well. They actually are looking at spirits all around them; they see very well, psychically. The mother then shakes a rattle and the baby starts focusing on his parents. It is the mother's job to be one of his guides in the physical world and it is her job to bond with him. As we go through life, we either learn to shut down, stay open, or hover somewhere in between. We tell all students who take our classes that it doesn't matter if *we* think they are psychic; it is important that *they* think they are psychic. We know they are!

Psychics have gotten such a bad reputation. People seem to be more accepting of people who use intuition or their sixth sense. But these kinds of people are not different from one another or from most other people. Our extra-sensory skills are vital to us. If we believe that God is all around us and within us, then in theory we believe that we are all one. The physical state that we are in, which contains ego, has a tendency to separate us from spirit. When we figure out that God is infinite and we are infinite because God made us in his likeness, then we sell ourselves short by thinking that we are anything less than we are. We are "in spirit" or inspired when we come to know and accept that we are one.

Our students work on these concepts and their abilities are enhanced by the time they are done with the classes. The development is natural. As the students will attest, attending our courses has bettered their lives. They feel more whole and lead their lives with more confidence. And for most, they do not do "psychic work." Rather, they use their psychic abilities in their daily lives! For some, the most valuable thing they take away is knowing that there is more to the universe than meets the eye, and for others, developing their psychic abilities chases away winter blues and other problems they experience when they are closed up.

The other benefit is that students notice synchronicities in their lives and then practice, for example, tuning into an open parking spot in the front of the store or the needs of their child or pet.

The answer to the second question is no. For me, I didn't get good responses from peers when I felt like I caused everything I saw. I was living my life, but not really accepting who I was. I did everything I could to deny my abilities, as many do. I believe that sometimes events are put into place to help us get back on track. And that is what happened to me. It took me seeing my brother's impending death and experiencing his death to open me up to recognizing more about myself.

Have you ever heard the saying "Sometimes someone has to hit rock bottom before they are willing to look up?" Well, I felt like I experienced just that. I was very blessed to have my brother in my life while he was alive, and from the other side he has helped me to know both my guides and myself. But seeing his death in a vision, and then having that vision come true was very difficult. I would not wish that experience on anyone!

And the answer to the question, "How long will it take?" is that it takes dedication and a degree of work that varies from person to person. Students generally get validations about their rate of progress in each of the classes, and after that, students usually experience a continued growth pattern as long as they continue the work.

We compare it to riding a bike; once you learn how to use your psychic abilities, you never really forget! It just gets pushed back in your memory, where it waits to be awakened.

As people age, some seek out religion and others will go on a quest to seek out mysteries of the universe. These are some reasons that students take our classes. For some, a traumatic event may have pushed them to seek answers.

Our students and clients fit into all of these categories. The most common denominator is that they seek knowledge and experience. Many have had a traumatic experience or feel a need to change their lives. And some are searching for the answer to the question "Is there more?"

We have taught students and had clients who are house-wives, husbands, psychologists, firemen, reporters, writers, professional people in a variety of businesses, widows, employment head-hunters, executives, and care-givers among many others.

We always share with our students that we learn as much from them as they learn from us. I would like to share with you some moments that our students have experienced.

One morning, on a day I had to teach, I received my regular 4 a.m. wake-up call. My guides have a great way of delivering early morning messages that tell me what I will need for the class that particular day. This one came on the morning of a weekend class in which we were teaching automatic writing and crystal gazing. I awoke to a vision of what happened when we were in Hawaii and Sylvia Browne shared her interpretation of Adam and Eve in the Garden of Eden. I could see her sitting there as she said, "Was Adam so stupid that he had to take the apple?" Now, I had no idea why I was seeing this, but as in the past, I was sure it would fit where it needed to fit.

In the class was a gentleman who was there out of curiosity. It was Sunday morning and, being a devout Catholic, he had been to mass that morning. Just before lunch break, I announced that, upon our return, we would be going right into the work on automatic writing and crystal gazing. The student raised his hand and asked, "In church this morning, the sermon was on temptation, so how do I know that this isn't temptation?" Of course, my thought was, "I now know who this morning's message is for."

I told the man, "When my guides came this morning, they shared with me the story of the Garden of Eden, and of Adam deciding to take the apple from Eve. You have studied with me now for what, three months? This is about you owning your own power and making your own decisions. If you feel you are uncomfortable with this in any way, I would be the first one to say: don't do it. Otherwise, you need to own your own decision of whether to participate or not." After lunch, he chose to participate and had some wonderful messages as a result. It was another validation of many things for him. This student is very proud of his development and holds his Catholic faith very close to his heart. He has learned that his beliefs fit together very well. It isn't what he lost; it's about what he has gained!

During another class activity, we were meditating. Upon coming out of their second meditation, I commented that one of the students needed to be less worried about her purse, because it was getting in her way of staying focused. Shocked, a student asked, "How did you know that?" I just smiled. We are upfront with our students. We let them know that we work together with their guides to help them wake up and remember what it felt like to be better connected with their guides. Her guide had let me know about her worries.

Students are often curious about how we do communicate psychically with them and with their guides in a large group. I explained that I raise my vibration and that they are attracted to it and therefore connect with me as we work through the day. If a student is not reaching, I just create more psychic energy or vibration to attract their attention until they do reach. By doing this, I am reading every one of them throughout the day, directly or with help from my guides and theirs. It helps me as a teacher assess where the teaching needs to go.

One day, I was describing the art of mediumship to a class and, as I looked at a woman in the class, I said, "You know, we will use her Grandma Mae as an example." The woman quickly retorted, "How did you know I have a Grandma Mae?" I replied, "Lucky guess." Receiving this kind of information is such an act of knowing for me that I am no longer second guessing myself. I find it humorous that our students point out things like this. It reminds me of me and the experiences I had with Sandy.

In another case, I had been invited to a student's house. We were almost done with a discussion when I asked her to check on one of her dogs. She asked why she should do it, and my reply was "I felt the dog has gotten out and is across the street." She looked out their living room window and the dog was sitting across the street, looking at her. She replied, "Now that is what I want to learn to do." I shared with her that messages are sent all the time; it is about listening and trusting what you get. I don't always do this, either. I am still a work in progress. God is not done with me yet.

As we work with our students, the learning goes two ways. We learn just as much as they learn. We see them question and challenge us, grow and learn with a willingness to explore their inner universes. It is amazing to watch each student move beyond merely hoping that there is more than what people usually experience, to knowing that there is more. When you add faith to that knowing, your life gets better.

Some students take only a few classes, and some take the whole series. When our students come to us, we expect a commitment on both sides to work hard. Each student will get out of the class what he or she choses to put into it. And for those who are committed, it is an experience they'll take with them through the rest of their life. Students, as a result of taking our classes, do a much better job making decisions in their lives. They learn to own their own power, recognize and become the author of their journeys, and create change in the world by changing themselves!

THE BOXES

*"Perhaps there will be one community when we
honor the freedom from within to choose our paths
based on the possibilities we see, and set the example by
awakening each day with the commitment to walk it
with less judgment and more compassion."*

What if things were just as they should be?

It wasn't long until I realized, through my experiences in
Florida at Starchild and with Mic and Patti, that I had been
living a rather rigid and judgmental life. I thought it was
normal. When you are so busy with your life and everything
around you is moving very quickly, it is easy to miss things.
The opportunity to see more usually shows itself in subtle
ways like synchronicities and coincidences, or it can be as
extreme as what happened to me with my brother's passing.

There are many books written about synchronicity,
coincidences, the manifestation of intentions, and other

related topics. They all show us what is possible. However, it is only when we allow ourselves to embrace the concept that we can learn less painfully, or change a painful lesson into an opportunity for growth, that we can begin to work from a positive space within us and evolve to see more of the possibilities that are open to us.

Opportunities present themselves constantly, every day. But many people, including me, hold themselves back and don't allow themselves the time to see the possibilities. In my case, I was spending a lot of energy just working to raise my children and be a wife, a grandma, a daughter, a sister, and whatever other roles I took on. But despite the worries of every day, and those about the past and the future, my psychic creativity still shone through at times. I'd see glimpses of more, but my attention was focused on just surviving my life and handling the responsibilities I had taken on.

When I describe this time of my life, I often say that I had created a box for myself, and was stuck in it. I still believe that living is a lot of work, and I am constantly creating different boxes that help me make sense of it all. I've learned, though, that I can exchange one box for another whenever I choose. This allows me to change my perspective and to move more fluidly through life and all of its turbulence.

For a long time, my take on the world was based on what I thought people should do to get through the difficulties that they'd encounter. I'd read the paper or listen to the news and think, "Well if they just…" or "They should do this…" or "If only this was…" In fact, I had so many responses that I can't even mention them all.

I remember Mic saying, "Things are just as they should be." I had a difficult time accepting this concept because so much about the world appeared less than perfect! I didn't realize at that time, that we create our lives and the shape of lessons that we face. They are lessons we might need to work through only once, or several times until we learn them. We continue this learning process because we are here to evolve.

When I started my journey through Sandy's classes, I thought, "Wow, I am so open!" "Yeah, right!" was the reply I heard from my brother, Wayne. The work I did with Patti and Mic helped me to understand how much I really have to learn. I believe my lesson plan is infinite. I now see why reincarnation makes sense. It would be hard to learn it all in just one or even two lifetimes. If you believe in a creator, then it would probably take many lives to become more like him! Anyway, I can see that this would be true for me!

Each one of us has our own story that we are weaving as we travel through this journey we call life. And yes, we touch other lives as we go. Our lives may be chaotic and out of balance at times, but this is merely a reminder that we have touched the inside edge of a box that we have created, and it is time to expand beyond it. And, by using our judgment to evaluate how we got into the middle of this chaos, we face the situation truthfully and with integrity. Only in this way can we see through the chaos. Facing chaos invites you to see more than you saw before. It can be a time of growth.

Working with my shaman friend, Mic, taught me just how layered we really are. Recall the boxes that we place ourselves in. Take a look at some of them: we establish boundaries around each country to separate one group of people from another. Religions establish doctrines and rules that function as lines of separation. People have been willing to die defending their "boxes" as the only right one and often they try to impose their boxes on others. Your family unit is a box, in a sense. To be conscious of this concept, and to always be watchful of your tendency to establish and embrace rigid thinking, helps you to create change more readily. The more we understand this, the more we will be able to expand a multi-cultural, global consciousness. Now that would be a big box.

When I was working through the concept of boxes and how we always try to make things fit, I was drawn to the concept of God. It led to creating a section in our class material in Inner Journey that we call "What are God's Possibilities?"

It refers to being in integrity with what we think God is. If God was—, then God would be— type theory. If God is infinite, then God would not be anything less. If God is omnipresent, then God would be everywhere—around us, in us—we would be one!

Can you see other possibilities?

SNAKE OIL
SALESMAN

"Freedom is a state of mind,
walking your walk is a state of presence,
for our choices represent us"

Recently I was having a conversation with someone who did not believe in psychics or healers. He commented that trusting them was for the "weak-minded." He told me a story of his father, a pharmacist on an island in the Caribbean. He said that psychics or healers would come into the store and want concoctions of ingredients to heal their clients' different ailments. His father would give the psychics and healers placebos, and they would pass the "potions" along to their clients and the clients would claim cures.

For some reason, the story and the comment about "weak-minded" people rolled around in my mind for some time. In my opinion, the "potions" his father made cured these people because they were so strong-minded and faithful. They were able to manifest their cure. The weak-minded people are the ones who chose not to see such opportunities. Weak-minded people are not those who believe in psychic phenomena, but are those who don't realize that the mind, body, and spirit are really one, with each part caring for the others.

I have heard countless stories about people who defy the medical community and live when they've been told that they are going to die. Christie was on a plane heading to Florida. She sat next to a woman who was diagnosed with terminal cancer. The doctors told her that she was going to die and there was nothing they could do. She chose to find a lifestyle that complimented her belief system, and she was living proof that people can be healed!

People generally have an easy time accepting that God is infinite and all-knowing. If God created us in His likeness as the scriptures say, then life is not a destiny or destination, but only something that is infinite. We are infinite beings just like God. And to be all-knowing is to understand everything. We must have the potential to understand everything. Life is a journey of evolution that spans over many lifetimes so that we can learn from our physical experiences how to take leaps of faith. Through all of this, we gain understanding of our higher selves.

It is when the physical body ages and weakens and can no longer be healed, that we experience the ultimate healing. Death is the ultimate healing because in death we shed diseased physical matter that no longer sustains life and can no longer serve as a vehicle for the eternal soul.

I can imagine the surprise a soul must feel when it realizes that it exists after death. When a spirit is set free, it must feel extremely light. After all, it has been carrying around the poundage of the physical body and the emotional weight of what it experienced. Being released, and understanding exactly what death means, must be exhilarating.

Our theory is that each person's infinite Higher Self has already manifested our death when we are born, by choosing to take on physical form. What a validation for each of us that we are manifesting or authoring our journey! This theory supports the fact that each person's Higher Self "knows" all the potential that the universe offers but we have to tap into this Higher Self in order to gain its knowledge. Rediscovering one's Higher Self is vital to one's ability to author one's journey at an ultimate level. After all, wouldn't you like to be up close and personal with someone who "knows"!

Remember, you are a part of Higher Self and Higher Self is you! This is the importance of making the time and effort to connect with our Higher Self on an at will basis rather than just tap into it on a hit-and-miss basis!

This is why I believe that embracing psychic phenomena is truly for the "strong-minded," the people willing to take responsibility for change in their own lives. And, although I understand the point of view of the man whose story opens this chapter, the "psychics" and "healers" he referred to were really "snake oil salesman." I found it amazing that this man readily accepted certain religious faith and the church, but wasn't open to the many different ways to understand the connection between our mind, body, and spirit. There are infinite ways to have faith in God.

For our students, following the leader is not an acceptable option. We encourage our students to take charge of their own lives and to make a difference. That means recognizing that, whether you are a Minneapolis fireman, a journalist, a homemaker, a computer expert, or a salesperson, you are part of a greater community and yet, you are the only you. Discover your strengths, strengthen your weaknesses, and walk your walk. Doing this will encourage others to do the same. I believe that realizing your psychic abilities is a result of knowing and centering yourself. And when we remember who we are when the body and spirit are integrated, we grow consciously.

Perhaps "remember who we really are" just means discovering the vastness of our inner existence and applying the knowledge of this discovery to our outer experiences. Can you envision the possibilities?

the ELUSIVE SIDE

*"I am aware of you, what touches your life and
how much you miss me. Are you aware of me?
There is a bridge that exists between two worlds;
it is a greeting card from heaven."*

There have been so many psychic mediums before me and there will be many more after I am gone. And as I listen to each client's and student's experiences, I see just how much the other side is communicating with us.

It is my belief that those on the other side communicate with us frequently, but that we are not always listening. We might ask ourselves, "Why would those on the other side try to get our attention?" Well, do you really think that those who have lived and walked this earth, and embraced family and friends, would lose interest in us? The answer for me is that, by the grace of God, a bridge exists and it is an expansive bridge that is intended to help support us, here in the physical.

When we choose to be aware of both the physical and the elusive world, we complete the connection between where we came from and where we will go. Our soul or spirit understands this. It is one of the steps in becoming one with yourself and one with the world. It changes lives and, for most of the people I know, it makes life better. We are never alone or deserted like a ship in the middle of an ocean with no engine or wind. This connection is what drives us and it is the wind beneath each of our wings. When we realize this connection, we are inspired. We paint, dance, sing, draw, or do whatever makes our hearts sing. We believe! It is the gift of our creation! It is you!

Imagine for a moment that your spouse or significant other passes away. You are an artist who feels uninspired because you are mourning the loss of your partner who brought witness to your life. All of a sudden, you start feeling the presence of this person. You perceive gentle reminders such as the smell of perfume, or feel their touch as you sit outside contemplating your life with them. Perhaps you hear a song on the radio that reminds you of the connection between this world and the other and, for that moment you smile and think, "Could it be a message?" It is, and know that this person has cleared away the baggage of their life, and that their presence still witnesses your life just as your thought witnesses theirs. It is a connection of spirit that is divine. It is elusive! Our love for each other transcends death, and I believe that heaven can be here on earth, in the elusive space that is the connection of souls, and the connection of our past, present and future.

Whether it is an ancient master, a guardian angel, a grandmother, spouse, or child, spirit guides come to us at different times in our lives, and our relatives come through to let us know that we are not alone and that our support system is never really lost but merely changed.

I was standing in a cemetery for a Memorial Day ceremony one year, and at his close the pastor said, "...and the hope that we will be reunited someday with those we have loved." I looked at Friar and he said, "What about the KNOWING that we will be reunited?" After all, if we believe that we will be once again reunited, then where do you think those who have passed are now? Just waiting? I don't know what it is like in your family, but for me, my grandmother, brother and dad didn't wait for much when they felt passionate about something. I can not fathom them just sitting around waiting! We have a vested interest in each other. Why wouldn't they want to help us and guide us?

Without the cares of the physical world, spirit can move in mysterious ways that can make our lives better and more whole.

Mic once shared with me that he believed there was nothing out there that wasn't for his highest good. I thought this seemed arrogant at the time, and I had to consider it a long time, like everything else, until I took from it what resonated with me. I now believe that whatever you believe is true for you. If you believe there is purgatory, you will be there. If you believe that ghosts can scare you or hurt you, you give that belief energy. When you believe that there is no spirit world, you are choosing not to see or hear it. Those things do or don't exist for you, depending on what you believe.

Friar has the patience of a saint. After all, he has stuck with me my whole life, through all the ups and downs, and through all the times I chose not to listen or pay attention. And he still hangs in there, even when I chose to take a step to the side rather than place one foot in front of the other. His love is unconditional and is displayed with compassion, grace, and wisdom. May we all achieve this state!

When my clients share that they can feel the elusive connection with the other side, I tell them that this is proof that those on the other side are communicating with us, and that, though we miss their physical presence, we can still feel their presence as they pass by or visit us in a dream. "Just say hello," I tell my clients. "Tell your loved ones that you think of them and that they are not forgotten!"

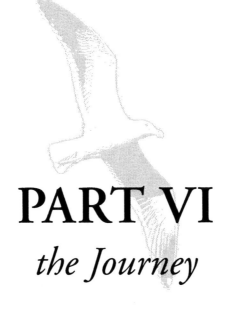

PART VI
the Journey

the
CHALLENGE

"Listen my children, for the most important messages
come from knowing there is more than we can see."

"Well if you are so psychic, then how come…" is probably
the most repeated phrase I hear when people ask me about
my work.

People who don't know what it is like doing this work
have a hard time understanding it. But hey, I can relate to
that. I was there!

First of all, let me reiterate that we are all psychic, it's just
that some of us choose to use our abilities more than others.
"Psychic," "parapsychology," "psychiatry," "psychology"; do
you notice the similarities in the words? It's psyche. We are
psychic beings, but for many it is easier to dismiss the things
that we can't explain fully than it is to try to understand them.
And yet, we all have psychic moments throughout our lives,

even those who are less open to them. Most of them are written off as coincidences and synchronicities.

Dr. Gary E. Schwartz has done work regarding spirit communication in a laboratory environment, using scientific equipment to measure different physiological readings of the medium and the sitter. HBO did a special on his work and the book he wrote called, *The Afterlife Experiments*.

Despite such efforts, the scientific community has a hard time theorizing things that can't be explained in physical terms. Communication between the spirit world and the physical world has been happening since humans came into physical being, and perhaps someday science will actually catch up to this concept! After all, until recently, science has understood only the physical world. But with its under-standing of quantum physics and other advancements, perhaps it is coming closer to understanding the more elusive aspects of our universe. Science is governed by theories and the theories, when repeated, become laws. But we need to remember that they are really only theories that are subject to change. Science itself has proven that!

Spirits can communicate with us loudly and clearly, or their communication can be more subtle and elusive. We just need to strengthen the bridge that connects us, whether it is through feelings, seeing, hearing, smelling, or tasting. This is easier said than done, since it is two-way communication between someone on the physical plane and someone on the non-physical plane. Each spirit has its unique vibration that can be recognized, just like a fingerprint. We have to raise our vibration and align our energy with that of the spirit. For many, this takes a lot of practice. Even when someone has the extra-sensory skills of sight or hearing, it isn't always easy to have clear communication. It takes a tremendous amount of energy to establish the connection and to hold it for long periods of time. The easiest kind of connection is in dreams, or when someone connects with his or her own relatives while in a relaxed state of mind.

One winter evening, I needed to go to the grocery store to fill the refrigerator before I left for Florida. I always tried to make sure that there was plenty in there for my husband when I was gone. Driving to the store, I heard Friar ask, "Are you sure you want to go shopping?" I said, "Yeah, I have to leave on a plane in the morning." This exchange repeated several times, but in my haste trying to get everything done, I didn't pay attention to what Friar was getting at. I didn't bother to ask, "Why do you ask?" But even when I didn't ask, Friar still tried a couple of times to ask the question.

Instead, I raced to the store, only to step out of the car, walk across the icy parking lot, and fall on my backside! Good move! As I was taken by ambulance to the emergency room, I thought of Friar's repeated question. I often wondered why spirits just don't say what they mean. Friar could have just said, "Hey, you! Do I have your attention? If you go to the store you are going to fall on your backside!" If he had, I wouldn't have gone! But no, spirits have got to do it their way. Why?

Guidance is just guidance. It is not meant to tell you what to do, or to do your work for you, but to guide you. I believe that spirits guide us with information that will provoke conversation, so we will choose to communicate with them. For example, when I first started this journey, they would talk to me, but if I pushed too hard, they would step back momentarily, as if to reel me in. I guess it makes it interesting. Personally, I wouldn't mind the "Hey, listen. If you go, you are going to fall. Watch what you are doing!" approach. Even if I heard this, I would still choose what I want to do! But I can't make my guides say what I want them to say. Just as we have free will, so do spirits. And we can always ask our guides for more information. This helps to make those connections stronger and stronger. The next time I will question Friar when he says, "Are you sure?" I will consider what he means more seriously. It was a painful lesson.

There are many times we are busy and aren't listening. But we can receive guidance by communicating with our guides, and we need to make an effort to make it work. To help make themselves more open to communication, our students work with mediation to center and balance themselves. And they use other techniques to keep themselves safe and protected.

I want to caution people reading this book that it is important to be smart. Get a psychic reading from someone with a good reputation. If a psychic requires you to come back every week for part of your readings, you should be suspicious.

A reputable psychic reader will tell you that you should use the information that you receive from a reading as a guide only to help you find your path. If the psychic gives you something that you do not like, see what you can do to get information for an alternative path. We tell our students that there are options—life flows and we have free will—and just because psychics "see" something about our future doesn't mean that we can't alter it by changing a behavior. We can!

Sticking to an ethical standard is essential, and here are some of the rules we teach our students and use ourselves:

We feel that a good psychic will first give you a little current information, so you can validate that the psychic is really receiving your information. The psychic should then go into issues that you can work through, and give you information about the future.

We suggest to our students that people receive readings only about once a year, unless they are in a transition and need guidance on particular issues. We feel that it isn't appropriate to connect with a person's spirit relatives on a regular basis so we use the rule no more than once a year.

In addition, we feel that a reputable psychic won't summon spirits. We don't do this. We merely communicate with whoever is around the client at the time of the reading. It is up to the client to say prayers and ask particular people to come through, if they hope to hear from them.

In addition, we teach our students to set their fees ahead of time and to clearly communicate their fees, and the services they offer, with clients before they begin a reading.

We teach our students to use the five-minute rule. With in the first five minutes, your client can cancel for any reason. There is no charge. The psychic is also allowed to cancel within five minutes if he or she feels uncomfortable reading someone.

Our clients are welcome to tape a private session. When possible, we will offer to tape the session for a nominal charge. Taping the session can be helpful, since it is often difficult to remember everything that happens during the session. Clients can continue to learn from their readings reviewing the session later.

When you are getting a reading, we recommend that you say nothing about your dead relatives. Let the psychic or psychic medium share the information with you. Only respond by a nod or smile to affirm something, and only answer what is directly asked. This responsibility is on you, the client! It is our desire that when people leave their readings, they feel like they truly received a reading and didn't just have the reader use volunteered information. Following these simple suggestions validates the reading! In readings a client may say, "Oh, yes, I know who that is. It's Bob, he was Grandma's favorite and I hope they are happy together." On the taped recording, I reply, "Well, you just gave me Bob's name, told me he was Grandma's favorite, and that Grandma has passed. Are you aware of that?" My goal is to give our clients clear, concise, verifiable information through validations and messages from those coming through. I make it clear to clients that information should not be volunteered. We ask that you answer only what is asked.

As a client, you should never feel pressured or coerced into making additional appointments or paying extra sums of money that had not been clearly agreed upon prior to the reading. If someone pressures you in this way, you should see red flags. Run, do not walk, to the nearest exit! You just found a scam artist!

However I do want to stress that there are many valid readers and a referral is just like getting a referral to an attorney or doctor. If someone else was really happy with what they received there may be a better chance you will be too!

We have information in the back of this book that includes good, reputable psychics, mediums, and healers. They work very hard and have integrity with their work.

I know that every one of them will give you an honest concise reading or a wonderful healing session. They are dedicated and experienced. Blessings to them and you!

COMMUNICATING
with GRACE

"Guidance is a gift to you from the heavens; to deny it is to deny self. But to walk with it is a gift; it is known as communicating with grace."

Reflecting on all that I've been through, I see the importance of grace and wisdom. In fact, I once asked one of my mentors, "How do you know when you have achieved grace and wisdom." He replied, "If you have to ask, you probably have already touched them."

Late in the first year of my journey, Christine and I were reading at a local psychic fair in a northern suburb of Minneapolis. We gave sample readings to a small audience, and then were available afterward to do private readings.

A man at a table close to ours was offering psychic readings. Christine and I thought we would each get a reading. When I went over to his table and sat down for my reading, he asked me what I wanted more than anything else. I said, "Grace and wisdom." He looked surprised and asked, "No, I mean what would really make your heart sing?" I looked at the frustrated young man and said, "Grace and wisdom."

He sighed and looked at me as he reached across the table in an attempt to pat me on the back. Again he asked, "No, I mean what would be the one thing that would make your heart sing more than anything else?" By now I was getting a little irritated with him and said, "Please keep your hands on that side of the table." (The back is the most receptive part of the body and a psychic doing a reading has no business reaching across the table to pat a person on the back.) After that I said, "I want grace and wisdom, for with that I would have everything! Would I not?" The man gave up and the reading ended.

I was astonished that something so uncomplicated could strike someone else as being so complicated. From my heart of hearts, I believe that having grace and wisdom would make my heart sing.

Communicating with Grace is a very fitting title for this book and it was given to me at one of the 4 a.m. wake-up calls. I had been wondering what a good name might be for this book and Friar just delivered the perfect one. He said, "Communicating with Grace."

Communicating with grace is our hope for the future. It is the groundwork needed so that we can live as a world community. It is a way that we can display compassion for people as members of a world community. It entails communicating with each other from a place of hope, a place that represents the way we want our world to be today and in the future.

What space can we create for future generations that represents divine grace and wisdom for everyone on this planet? What would your ideas be? Perhaps you see a place where life is valued and treated so sacredly that destroying it is never taken lightly, where life is never traded or sold! I can see a place where communication between people is clear and people treat one another with dignity and compassion, where people are not looked down on or judged for their choice of religion. We really can choose to be the change that we want for our world. Some people may feel that what I see is an altruistic world but, it is what I choose to manifest. Manifesting it through open communication, compassion, understanding, and applying a little grace and wisdom. This means you take all of the above and create in yourself what you see and then merely reach your hand out. It is up to someone to see theirs and reach their hand out, will they? Choice! It is theirs and yours. You be your change and it is bound to spread on its own merit!

We need to evolve if we want to communicate with grace. When we bridge both worlds, we can work from a higher heart space, and open the door so that we can receive the wisdom we need in order to succeed and be who we really are. Communicating with grace opens the gateway to realizing that, as physical beings, we are not separate from our spirit, and our spirit is not separate from our physical body. We are all one and of one.

No single master such as Jesus or Buddha "formed" a religion. They simply walked this earth living their lives and sharing what they KNEW. Humans formed religions and humans teach through those religions their own interpretations of the masters. I find it sad that people often believe that theirs is the only way, when religions share so many core ideas. Perhaps there is a clue in this: perhaps all these masters walked under one God. Choosing a religion is an act of choice; living a religion is an act of faith.

Dear Reader:

The next time you feel the hair on the back of your neck or on your arm stand up, or feel a gentle breeze when no window is open, or have a dream that is a vivid reminder of someone you love who has passed away, or hear an answer to a prayer, remember that you just "Communicated with Grace." Smile, say thank you, and know that you are loved and never alone.

With Love and Guidance,

Susan Anderson

for more
INFORMATION

You can contact us at:

Bridging Two Worlds®
% Introspect…A Look Within
P.O. Box 8464
Minneapolis, MN 55408

To book a private reading or event, for lecture or tour information, class schedules, or other inquiries, please call or visit our website!

612-824-2427

Bridging Two Worlds® ticket information: 941-587-8550

www.bridgingtwoworlds.net

Drawing by **Charles A. Filius**

REFERRALS

J. Lydia Clar
Psychic Readings
P.O. Box 410636
Melbourne, FL 32941-0636
Phone: (321)253-6156
Website: www.lydiaclar.com

Glenn Dove
Spirit Communication
P.O. Box 701
Baldwin, NY 11510
Phone: (516)223-2567
Website: www.glenndove.com

Pat Kalouza
Astrology
3309 31st Street South
Minneapolis, MN 55406
Phone: (612)724-4128

Patti A. Star, LMT
The School of Essential Oil Studies
Sarasota, FL
Phone: (941)356-7768
Email: visionsmrk@aol.com
Website: www.AromatherapyOne.com

BIBLIOGRAPHY

Eakins, Pamela, and illustrator Joyce Eakins. *Tarot of the Spirit* and companion cards *Tarot of the Spirit*. Boston: Weiser, 1992.

Edward, John. *One Last Time*. New York: Berkley Books, 1999.

Edward, John. *Understanding your Angels and Meeting your Guides.* Carlsbad, CA: Hay House, 2000.

Edward, John. *Unleashing Your Psychic Potential.* Hay House, 2000.

Schwartz, Gary E., William L. Simon, and Linda G. Russek. *The Afterlife Experiments.* New York: Atria Books, 2002.

Waite, A.E., and Pamela Colman Smith. *The Rider Tarot Deck.* Stamford, CT: US Games Systems, 1989.

About the AUTHOR

Susan Anderson is a nationally recognized psychic medium, teacher, author, and lecturer. She has done many public performances, readings, and lectures. Susan can be heard on radio stations nationwide. Susan and her daughter, Christine wrote *Inner Journey: The Series*© and are actively teaching the series and applying the self-development, motivational and psychic aspects of these teachings in their public events called *Bridging Two Worlds*®.

> *"Susan is Amazing. I've had listeners call back crying, saying she totally nailed it. All of their questions were answered without them even being asked."*
> –Josh Reno, morning show producer for KRBE, Houston, TX

Susan lives with her husband and their border collie, Gracie, in Minneapolis, MN. She has three grown children and eight beautiful grandchildren who live in the area. She is currently working with her daughter, expanding the adult curriculum and is writing another book.